THE
SEVEN-DAY
SOUL

Finding Meaning
Beneath the Noise

For information on workshops and speaking
engagements please visit
www.susannahhealy.com

THE SEVEN-DAY SOUL

Finding Meaning Beneath the Noise

Susannah Healy

HACHETTE
BOOKS
IRELAND

First published in 2019 by Hachette Books Ireland

A CIP catalogue record for this title is available from the British Library.

ISBN 978 1 47368 516 1

Gestalt image on page 19 © Peter Hermes Furian/Shutterstock.com
Typeset in Sabon by redrattledesign.com

Printed and bound in Great Britain by Clays Ltd, Elcograf S.p.A.

Hachette Books Ireland policy is to use papers that are natural, renewable and recyclable products and made from wood grown in sustainable forests. The logging and manufacturing processes are expected to conform to the environmental regulations of the country of origin.

Hachette Books Ireland
8 Castlecourt Centre
Castleknock
Dublin 15, Ireland

A division of Hachette UK Ltd
Carmelite House, 50 Victoria Embankment, EC4Y 0DZ

www.hachettebooksireland.ie

To my parents, John and Miriam, my husband Arthur
and our three boys, Arthur, Oliver and Chester.

My meanings

My joys

I love you

Thank you

Contents

1

More Than a Feeling

The Nature of Spirituality

Several years ago, I attended a day-long mindfulness workshop in a city-centre retreat house in Dublin. The event was held in a warm and cosy room with walls lined with books on mindfulness, Buddhism, and wisdom from all the world's faith traditions.

The retreat was led by a Catholic nun who I knew had dedicated her life's work to the poor, and in particular, to the homeless. Knowing the sister's work in advance, I was a little surprised when we arrived at the end of the day without her ever having made reference to the history of mindfulness in the Catholic Church. If I'm honest, I was a little put out that my 'territory' had not been defended.

I approached the sister privately as everyone was leaving, and asked her why she had not felt the need to mention the history of mysticism in the Catholic Church, given that she had dedicated her life to its teachings. Her answer was as profound as it was simple. She turned to me and said, 'There are many ways to God.'

These words have stayed with me ever since. Here was a woman who was giving all her life in service to God through the Catholic Church, but she was able to leave aside any egotistical need to convince herself or others that the path she followed was the right or only way of coming to live a spiritual life. Her life-changing words showed a spiritual maturity full of love and openness; one that did not search for the approval of others, but instead recognised the expanse of spirit that surrounds us – the width, and breadth, and breath of our daily lives.

The spiritual dimension is everywhere, all the time. Its existence does not depend on our attention, nor does it come and go into being according to the rise and fall of our beliefs. It is Being itself – the 'is-ness' of all things – the inner life of the visible world that offers itself to us to be known and lived amongst.

The spiritual aspect of our universe is not some detached or cloud-like feeling that would have us float above 'real' life – the kind of place that we'd have to leave in order to return to 'reality'. It is the very essence of reality, the truest and most thorough knowing of reality which, by way of divine plan or the limits of human perception, we find difficult to see.

Many of us will have had moments when we were

able to experience this depth to the world, this other way of seeing. But for most of us, these times are fleeting, interrupted by the rush of things to be done and to do. Hurriedness can seem like the enemy of a spiritual life when we look upon spirituality as just a feeling. Certainly, stillness makes it easier for us all to feel connected to our personal higher power. But when we expand our understanding of spirituality to be a way of living, then we can look upon every moment as an opportunity to live a more spiritual life. In *The Seven-Day Soul*, we explore this breadth of our spiritual selves in the days and doings of our lives.

Spirituality is the dimension of ourselves that wants to understand the big existential questions about life, such as why are we here? And what is the meaning and purpose of my life? Spirituality is the self-transcendent aspect of life – the part that goes beyond the outline of our physical body; and that looks at the larger context of our existence in relation to things that are outside of ourselves, including connection to others and our place in the universe, and for some, connection to a transcendent reality such as God, Allah or Ultimate Mystery.

Spiritual matters are the 'big picture' questions that require a broader lens on life than we usually use in everyday living; the 'seeing the wood for the trees' perspective. The beliefs that we arrive at about this ultimate reality, about the larger context of our living, then become our explanatory narrative that guides our living and our dying. Thus spirituality is the map of life we draw for ourselves.

'Bloom Where You Are Planted'

Like so many Irish people, I was brought up in the Catholic faith; and despite ongoing struggles with some of the most basic teachings, I retain a strong belief in God.

When in adulthood I began to practise mindfulness meditation, and then trained as a mindfulness trainer, I sometimes struggled with what seemed to me like the absence of any recognition of a higher power. The mindfulness that is popular and widespread today is a secularised version, abstracted from its deeply spiritual Buddhist roots.

Spiritual practises such as stillness, compassion, and seeing the world with wonder, are key teachings in the secularised mindfulness programme, but even these eventually came to be not enough for me. I needed to acknowledge my belief in something greater, which I call God, but many know in other ways as Goddess, Love, Ultimate Mystery, Yahweh, Brahman, Mother Earth, or by its numerous other names.

There is a story told that a seeker from the Western world once approached the Dalai Lama and asked to be taught the ways of the Buddha. But the Dalai Lama turned to him and said, 'Bloom where you are planted.'

When we struggle with our own traditions, it can be very appealing (and also educational) to look to other traditions for inspiration. But as the sister at my mindfulness retreat had pointed out, these traditions are all just variations on our journey towards ultimate truth. That is not to say that they are all interchangeable or replaceable by one another. But each of them puts demands and disciplines upon us that aim to teach us to discover the depths and hidden heights of the world around us – to see more clearly what is already here: the underpinnings, or undercarriage, of existence.

Blooming where I was planted for me meant looking towards the mystical Christian tradition and its teachings on meditation and contemplation, as well as other traditions. Meditation and variations on mindfulness can be found in nearly all the world's faiths, and also in secular and atheistic spirituality. But what was really a revelation to me was the new images of God which these mystical teachings offered me. I found them to be full of awe, and recognition of the sacredness of all things, but at the same time offering an alternative – or perhaps an additional – way of knowing God personified as the old man in the sky, to whom we've attributed all of our whims, jealousies and weaknesses.

Dipping into these texts, I was being offered what was for me a much 'holier' version of God. Stillness, compassion, and seeing the world anew were still taught to be key elements in any meditation and prayer practise, but now with the recognition of a higher power with even greater height.

These mystical teachings challenge traditional images that we often have of God, an image which for some is too difficult to believe in. This new aspect of my Christian faith gave meditation back to me in a way that felt truly authentic and my own. It opened up ways of prayer that were no longer filled with someone else's words, and were instead sometimes utterly silent. It gave renewed reason to my mindfulness practise, laying it in context of my own traditions. It gave me a map of meaning and new territories to explore in my spiritual life. And importantly, it reminded me how to see the daily hassles and chores of my life in relation to that spiritual reality.

Of course we will be pushed towards and pulled away from this sense of sacredness in everyday life over and over again. But when we learn to brush our teeth, dress the kids, send an email, cook the dinner, commute, maintain relationships, and all the other things we do in our busy lives, with the intention of trying to live in relation to whatever we consider ultimate truth, then we are hard at work in building a better version of ourselves – a life lived out in the continuous awareness of our values. It is inevitable that we will fail again and again. We will say things we shouldn't, get impatient, act selfishly and all the rest. But it's like learning any new skill – we've got to put in the training. What we do, we become.

Noticing, or gaining awareness, is the first thing that needs to happen to make a change. Our meditation or prayer practise then literally becomes our way of practising what we want to become more of. To try over and over is to reorient ourselves, towards a way of living that we value and aspire to.

Personal, Not Private

Blooming where we are planted can feel like an uphill battle, and sometimes a solitary one. Spirituality is generally considered to be a private matter, and it isn't often that the spiritual aspect of ourselves is acknowledged in public life.

Just as it is rare to hear a politician speak about our need to create a meaningful workplace as they cut the ribbon on a new office block, we do not hear an architect designing a streetscape stopping to consider our needs for silence, or to commune with 'something greater'; nor a doctor ask about our beliefs when faced with anything other than a life-threatening diagnosis. Yet as we will see in later chapters, psychological and biomedical research shows that spirituality is a fundamental aspect of good health, alongside care of the body and mind. Many of us may avoid bringing up spiritual matters in conversation with friends because it feels too much like we are prying into personal matters. But in doing so we mistake what is personal for what is private. Spirituality is deeply personal, but it is not a private matter.

Each of us has a role – in fact a responsibility – to build ourselves a more compassionate world; and to put in the work that not only makes life more meaningful now, but also prepares us for the times we are really tested.

The times we gently encourage a child to see another person's perspective, or patiently explain their homework to them again; when we stop to help a tourist struggling with a map on the street, say no to another plastic bottle, copy someone in on an email to make them feel included, are grateful for having work to do, and actually notice the sun has gone down – these can all be ways of living in connection to a bigger picture, developing in each of us a deeper connection to our Seven-Day Soul.

Not Just on Sundays

Building our spiritual life is done moment by moment, as each tiny brick of eternity presents itself to us. Very often we can be tempted to mentally box it off for Sundays, yoga classes, weekends, retreats or times of prayer. All of these are valuable, structured ways of preparing the soil for us to bloom. But they are not meant to stand alone and separated from the rest of our daily living. They are meant to *inform* our daily living.

We don't go to the gym to be good at going to the gym, but to be fit in life. In a similar way, formal spiritual practises are meant to help us to live our lives in a new way. In a more conscious way – living with intent. Spirituality then is not so much the dreamy, disconnected cloud-like warm feelings that we can sometimes enjoy, but more an intentional, active, directed and disciplined way of living every moment in relation to a dimension of reality that some of us intuit but cannot see. It is the ongoing project of evolving our part in the collective consciousness of humanity towards whatever we consider to be sacred, known in some religious traditions as enlightenment, putting on the mind of Christ, or pulling back the veil of Maya.

Seen in this light, spirituality is wiping a nose lovingly, caring for wild animals during winter months, and biting our tongue when we feel like biting back. All of these moments give us the chance to build our spirituality muscle, to grow spiritually stronger through the sometimes dull repetitions of everyday challenges. In doing this we imbue our lives with meaning by taking our place in building a better world.

As we will see in the coming chapters, these practises will also create a new model of wellbeing for us that includes our spiritual dimension; a model that might otherwise collapse like a two-legged chair if left to balance on the pillars of mind and body alone.

Reintegrating spirituality into our personal lives,

and into the public life that we build together, has to start by bringing to conscious awareness that which we normally allow to remain unconscious, to help us see clearly how we are already, and to understand the different modes of mind available to us – as well as how to use them.

Throughout the book you will find some practical ways you can integrate spirituality and meaning into your day. *The Seven-Day Soul* offers you a template of how to live a more spiritual life, with a theme to focus on for each day of the week. Each of us must hold the bar high for ourselves, challenging ourselves to grow beyond our habitual ways of being. There is a better world available to us when we challenge ourselves to not do as we always do, but to grow to be a better version of ourselves and all that we can be.

2

Perception Deception

Questioning the Map

'Every man takes the limits of his own field of vision for the limits of the world.'
– Arthur Schopenhauer, *Studies in Pessimism*

As we set out to develop our Seven-Day Soul we need to first notice that we already have a habitual way of seeing the world – a sort of lens on everything we see that forms our take on reality.

This lens is formed by our personality, our parents, our experiences and the culture we live in. It affects how and what we attend to, and what we value and nurture. But when our lenses on the world become unconscious and ingrained, they are often handed down through generations, creating an almost worldwide act of groupthink from which it can be difficult to escape.

Tides of Thought: Scientism

Our entire body is a living lens, an interpretive centre through which we filter existence by way of our paltry five senses. Like the fish who doesn't see the water, each of us lives, works and does in a cultural zeitgeist that we are often blind to. When the entire community, family, workplace, country or continent in which we live operates within the same values and outlook, it becomes very hard for us to notice those values as options among a range of any number of possible choices.

Scientism is one such cultural lens on our view of the world. The belief that science will eventually answer all our questions may or may not be true, but it ignores the ability to notice that scientific findings depend on the questions we ask. We may be looking in the wrong place. The scientist from another era who weighed a body before and after death to discover the 'weight' of the soul was blind to the assumption made in the question he asked; namely, that the soul is a 'thing'. The method of measuring pre- and post-death were perfectly logical and scientific, but the basic assumption was (we now think) mistaken. The unconscious assumption in the scientist's research was based on what has become known as a 'God-of-the-gaps' theory.

'Each person sees the world not as it is but as he or she is. When he opens his mouth to describe what

**he sees, he in effect describes himself,
that is, his perception.'**
— **Stephen R. Covey,** *The Divine Center*

God-of-the-gaps is the outdated belief that God was to be found in the parts of the universe and the body that science had not yet explained. Whatever we couldn't understand – such as dark matter in space, and the many parts of neuroscience we can't get to grips with – were God's territory.

The problem with this idea is that as scientific understanding progressed, God found Himself (Herself or Itself) standing on a postage stamp-sized piece of the universe. This view meant that if it could be explained, it couldn't also belong to God. The concept was dualistic, separating matter from the sacred, so that God – or whatever we might consider divine – had no place in the scientifically explainable, material world. Such an approach smacked again of 'old man in the sky' imagery of God, and led to such unhelpful phrases as 'the God particle'; once it was found it was no longer God's particle.

These mental models of how we see the world – the separation of the soul from the rest of the body, the belief in God as a thing, the inclusion of meaning in our vision of health, and so on – direct how we interact with ourselves, others and the world. The mechanistic approach of breaking down the natural world into parts which can be individually investigated has been useful in so many ways in helping us to better understand the world. But such an approach cannot observe each part in relation to another, and it ignores the relationship of that part to a larger whole. An atomistic lens of looking at the world is not wrong as long as we are conscious of using it, so that we may at another time choose a wider-angled lens to look at each piece in relationship with the system it operates in.

The interconnectedness of humanity and nature was a fundamental aspect of ancient teachings, from Aristotle, Plato, the ancient Egyptians, the Stoics and other teachings. The Hindu Vedas, the Qur'an, and Christianity all speak of the unity of all Being in different ways. Stoic philosophy taught that 'right knowledge' could only come about by living in agreement with nature, or an inter-relatedness between the truth of things, thought and action.

St Thomas Aquinas, writing in the middle ages, proposed a cosmology of an 'Eternal Law', and Hindu writers of an 'Ever-living Law' (Sanatana Dharma). The creator was not separate from his creation, and sacredness was to be found in all of nature. But as HRH the Prince of Wales points out in his book *Harmony*, this positioning of divinity within nature began to break down during the thirteenth century, when the collective perception of God changed from positioning Him within nature to outside of it. This gave rise to questions which we still ask today, such as: Does God intervene in the world? Is He a personal God? Such questions would never have been asked when God was within nature.

The decoupling of God and nature allowed humanity to do what it wished with nature, which began to be seen as something that needed to be controlled, not partnered. It caused us to need words like 'supernatural', as opposed to seeing everything, even the unexplainable, as part of nature.

The new paradigm of separation of humanity and nature increased in the seventeenth century, after mathematician and philosopher René Descartes suggested that scientific exploration should look at each separate element of the mechanism of the world in order to understand it. Descartes was a religious man, but still felt that the world could be understood mechanistically, separate from religious and philosophical beliefs. This came to be known as Cartesian dualism which, although hugely useful in some ways, led to the separation of body and mind in medicine, an idea we are only beginning to overcome.

Images of God fall foul of what we could call the preposition problem – the limitations of our language. If we don't have a word for something, we can't imagine it. And if we can't imagine it, we don't make a word for it. 'God' is a word that comes with many additional associations, most notably the idea of God as a man, or a thing with an outline that could hypothetically be drawn.

Logically but unconsciously, we then need to place Him somewhere, because if He is a thing, then He must be somewhere. So when God became separated from nature and was no longer *in* nature, then our minds jumped to the conclusion that He is *outside* of nature.

Variations on this theme are offered, such as: God (or the divine) is outside of nature but we see His work in nature, or God is back in nature, but only in humanity, and so on. Further metaphors are offered concerning whether we are created by God, are part of God, or contain part of God.

All of these metaphors are useful teaching tools, but they can only be stretched so far. Our vocabulary is limited to what our five senses can decipher out of the soup of signals that surrounds us in the atmosphere. But the mystery that we are speaking of is not limited by language, nor is it human. It does not rely on our comprehension or belief for its existence. In the Vedic tradition, the illusion of separation from oneness experienced by human beings is due to what is called the 'veil of Maya'.

Maya is a sort of cosmic illusion, the power in creation that causes us to see duality, me and other, as being separate. Most world wisdom traditions, theistic and atheistic, have a similar teaching on duality as being a trick of, or lacking in, our human consciousness, which is overcome in death or by enlightenment.

Perhaps the starting point in unhitching ourselves from our habitual ways of how we see ourselves and how we fit into the bigger context of the world is to begin by recognising the limitations of language.

'**Most people never question their maps. They assume that's the way it is. They don't hold viewpoints; their viewpoints hold them.**'
– **Stephen R. Covey**

Science and spirituality are commonly presented as an either/or scenario, where people tend to describe themselves as being either spiritual or scientifically minded. But science and spirituality are different ways of encircling the same thing; different methods of gathering different types of findings. And because of our cultural preference for things that can be measured with the scientific methods we have discovered so far, the topic of spirituality is sidelined, or presented in extreme or alternative ways that do not give a fair explanation of the relevance of spiritual matters to everyday life.

The abstract and unknowable nature of spirituality doesn't fit well with the scientific preference for collation of facts and figures. But if the division between science and spirituality could be imagined as not being able to see the wood for the trees, then we might better be able to understand that all 'trees' of scientific endeavours exist within the 'woods' of spirituality.

Spirituality is the constant backdrop, the scene in which great scientific endeavour takes place. It is about our place in relation to the widest context of all, and a life lived in relation to that. Spirituality's focus of study is the dual nature of our divine within and its place in the all-encompassing, the universal, the all-that-is. By design, scientific measurement must narrow down its focus of enquiry in order to collect accurate measurements. To best understand our big-picture universe, we need to utilise the lenses of both empirical measurement and other ways of knowing.

Figure and Ground, the Gestalt

Gestalt is a school of psychology that studies the way we perceive things visually. It suggests that we direct our attention to things in our visual field that stand out, rather than towards the background setting. This has become known as 'figure and ground' theory, with 'figure' meaning the things that stand out from the background, which is the 'ground'. It refers to our tendency to identify a foreground and a background.

We do this unconsciously by grouping certain things together when they are near each other, or seem similar, connected, continuous, or to form a pattern. In this way, so the theory goes, our mind makes sense of a chaotic world. It is every marketing specialist's dream that their product becomes the figure, standing out from the ground of the countless similar products on the shelf. Gestalt psychology isn't normally associated with religion or spirituality, but perhaps it should have been. As a study of attention and perception, it is in fact highly relevant to the conversation of spirituality, meaning and purpose.

An example of the 'figure and ground' of Gestalt psychology. The viewer who regularly plays chess or has a love of gardening might see a chess piece or an ornate garden vase as being the 'figure', while someone else might see two opposing faces as 'figure' and the central space as 'ground'.

When we are under pressure to pay the bills, get somewhere on time, prepare for work tomorrow, get to the airport on time, or look after livestock or a sick family member, these urgencies become our figure that fully fills our span of attention. This leaves little or no space for us to consider the larger context we live in – the spiritscape of our lives.

Spirituality is a macro lens on our lives. It is not separate or distant, but includes the realities of our existence in a larger picture. Our jobs, roles, ups and downs, birth, life and death are all seen in relation to something bigger, where the ground comes more fully into view.

If you take a second now to notice that you are reading, you come into the present moment. If you now visualise your life from birth, stretching forwards in time, you have expanded your lens to incorporate a larger context; perhaps you are reading because it is relevant to your studies, or because you have developed an interest in spiritual matters in adulthood. This becomes the context in which you are reading. Spirituality includes and expands this context to an even larger 'ground', where your whole life becomes lived in relation to something personally meaningful.

In naturalistic spirituality, the life (figure) is lived on the ground of love or nature. In theistic spirituality, the ground is love and a divinity. This difference in selecting what is background and foreground in life is the basis of the psychological and health benefits associated with spiritual living, where even suffering can be interpreted as having a purpose – a larger context. The patient with lots of visitors can be company to the patient who has none. When looking beyond the attention-grabbing immediacy of suffering, the widower can view his loneliness as saving his deceased wife the suffering he endures, had she outlived him.

In order to introduce new ways of seeing the world, that can also integrate findings from various aspects of science, we have to begin to look at our beliefs, or what we consider 'givens', more as tides of thought of our generation or our culture, rather than actual facts about the world. We need to stop equating our spirituality with our psychology; they are both important, and certainly interrelated, but they are different aspects of who we are. Spirituality must relate to something more than its perception in the brain, or it is simply psychology. What we need instead is a way of blending what we have learned from science with the commonalities in teachings of ancient wisdom traditions.

'Everything we hear is an opinion, not a fact.
Everything we see is a perspective, not a truth.'
– Marcus Aurelius, Emperor of Rome,
First Century AD

The Second Tide of Our Day: Secularity

In *Beyond Religion*, the Dalai Lama comments that in India the word 'secular' means all faiths and none. In the West, it just means none. Certainly for some, secularity means a focus on the material world without judgement on spiritual matters, either positive or negative. Others take secularity to mean a negation of a spiritual dimension to the world. Which form of secularity are we choosing for our society? Are we really adopting a philosophy of 'each to their own'?

As an underlying intention, the philosophy of each to their own is a noble and inclusive one. But when secularity is interpreted to mean not every wisdom tradition (and atheism) but instead none, it draws a bland common pathway which misses the richness of the surrounding spiritual landscape that it is afraid to acknowledge for fear of causing offence. With the rise of a secularism devoid of any spirituality, we seem to have lost our sense of the sacred, be that nature, God or the universe. We seem to have lost awe.

• • • • • • • • • • • • • • • On Reflection • • • • • • • • • • • • • • •

Your Life on Canvas

If you were to draw or paint your daily life on a giant canvas, what might act as the backdrop for everything you do in your day? Are there values or beliefs that you might write in large lettering across the background canvas? Do you have a mental image of your life's purpose, or foundational beliefs that provide the root system of your actions? When we look at the activities that fill our days from this vantage point, we can see every moment as a means to live out the values that we choose for ourselves and as opportunities to develop our Seven-Day Soul.

3
Images of God
Love's Coat of Many Colours

'God created man in His image and likeness
And man returned the compliment.'

— Unknown

How Did We Get Here?

The German philosopher Martin Heidegger once said that language is the house of Being. It creates our reality and sets boundaries on what we see and what we speak about.

Our vocabulary develops from experience; our own and that of others. What we can create, imagine or know through our senses is ascribed a name, or a word to describe it. But we forget that a word is just a symbolic representation, a useful symbol that allows us to communicate our ideas with others. The four-legged structure with a flat top that I sit at is not a 'table', any more than it is 'una mesa' or 'une table'. Each of these words is simply a way for us to communicate what we are referring to with others, but no one could argue that one is more correct than the others. Language is symbolic, and as such is limited – it is always the shortened version of the thing it speaks of.

Religious But Not Spiritual?

As soon as we try to describe God – or whatever we believe to be the divine, ultimate reality, or the final explanation of all things – we set limitations upon it.

Many Christians arrive into adulthood with an image of God as a kindly old man in the sky who the believer will meet in an afterlife. This image is one which most of us were given in early childhood, and few further developments of this image were offered after this time. The individual is then left to face the uncomfortable question of whether or not they still believe in God as this image; or if there are other, perhaps not alternative so much as simultaneous ways of relating to God.

In the West, many people have lapsed from membership of organised religion. For some, the discoveries of science bequeathed us with too little left to believe in. When the parts of our world that could not be explained by science became less and less, many people felt they no longer needed a spiritual dimension to their lives, and as empirical explanation replaced divine mystery. Others felt that they could meet their spiritual needs better outside of organised religion.

Of those who stayed, most truly believe, but there are probably some who could possibly be described as 'religious by rote'. Some are engaged enough to want to hold out for more understanding; some are perhaps more stuck, rather than holding on. Of those who left the church, some lost belief in God or a higher order completely. But for most, the loss of membership of organised religion gave way to a new identity as being what is often referred to as Spiritual But Not Religious (SBNR).

The Lie of Language

Overly anthropomorphic imagery of what God might look like can provide us with a sense of familiarity, but when it fails to do so, it can be the biggest cause of loss of faith. It can be the big divider that people often say they found too hard to believe in. But anything we say about God, the absolute, or ultimate reality will always be limited by language, because that which we speak of is language-less.

As we have seen, our lexicon limits us to a set number of prepositions and adjectives which we can use to describe something; in our human world, something either is or isn't; it can be in, through, on, over, under, outside of, and so on. But everything must be one of these things.

God, as we imagine Him, It or Her, also has to fit into one of these descriptors. Once described, we pray, beg, cajole Him, ascribing God human emotions such as anger, wrath, and moods that can be swayed and charmed into answering our prayers. We add to Him an ego that requires us to believe in Him. We use Him like a vending machine in the sky to answer our prayers. We try to bottle God, to have Him for our own.

Images of God can alter with the zeitgeist of a culture. Over the past century, different Christian generations have focused on an 'Almighty Father' in a more patriarchal 'God-fearing' society wearied by war, and a 'loving Jesus' who washed the feet of sinners as societal hierarchies flattened and individualism became the public mood. We later reinstated God the Father, this time as a loving grandfather figure – the loving old man in the sky image. In more modern times, the slightly more gender-neutral Holy Spirit seems more in keeping with the culture. But each of these can offer us different ways of encountering the one and the same God for the Christian believer.

Teachings and attitudes to the Virgin Mary have also changed, from a focus on her virginity as being her greatest quality, to valuing her strength of character in enduring the suffering and death of her only son. It is probably the case that the traditional idea of praying to the Virgin Mary for her intercession on the person's behalf has disappeared as society's hierarchies flattened. We feel comfortable speaking directly to God in a society that has not been raised to be 'God-fearing'.

For both religious individuals and those who still believe in God but do not consider themselves religious, the problem isn't trying to agree on a gender-neutral title or phrase that ticks the box for us all. The real issue lies in the failure across religions to educate practitioners in the shortcomings of making mental symbols of God. Despite the fact that many mystics, as we will see in later chapters, describe the unknowability of God, most Western organised religions have continued to offer a very human image of God. Our own minds complete the picture.

Whatever our religious background, most of us have not been made privy to more abstract ways of knowing God, which are remarkably similar across all faith traditions. Traditional hierarchical approaches to religion have operated on the basis that people were not able to deal with more abstract concepts and therefore needed a clear-cut, or concrete, image of God – in keeping with the one they were first offered in childhood.

Historically, going back centuries, this may have been appropriate, when there was a vast gap in the education of clerics and laity. But religious art, and depictions still used today, continue these externalised models of God, as a man on a cloud in the sky, or the Holy Spirit as a white dove. And yet, a look at the writings of Christian theologians shows that they worked hard to deconceptualise God, using such phrases as 'The Cloud of Unknowing' and 'the Ground of our Being' to undo the 'draw-ability' of God – God with a physical outline. Even the Catechism of the Catholic Church refers to this:

> *We must therefore continually purify our language of everything in it that is limited, image-bound or imperfect, if we are not to confuse our image of God – 'the inexpressible, the incomprehensible, the invisible, the ungraspable' – with our human representations. Our human words always fall short of the mystery of God.*

This limitations of words to describe what we have come to call God is also expressed in the Tao: 'The Tao that can be expressed is not the Eternal Tao.'

These limited images of God have also given rise to the question that never goes away: 'If God exists, and is a loving God, why do bad things happen?' Various answers have been offered over the centuries, such as God's will, punishment, or being part of a divine plan that we will understand in the afterlife. But these answers are based again on the belief of the God who remains in the sky. If we were to instead try to invoke God as a way of us dealing with such situations, a way that has an interiority about it (God or divinity within us), but which is also connected to God or an outer vastness far beyond our comprehension, our relationship with God changes.

This, of course, is just another model, but one in which God is lived through our actions and experiences, inextricably linked to the greater world that exists outside of us, in all its mystery and potential. When we recognise the interiority of God within ourselves, we take up the reins of responsibility in a new spiritual life – one where we can be powerful agents of love and a lived spirituality.

More than anything, what we need is to be given the space for our doubts to exist without feeling that we are failing, or that we are losing our religion – without seeing our relationship with spirituality as a zero-sum game. To allow doubt and unknowing to be part and parcel of the spiritual journey is an admission that certainty is not a bulwark against being wrong, and that doubt is an inherent aspect of an evolving spiritual life.

> **'Doubt is not a pleasant condition,**
> **but certainly is an absurd one.'**
> **– Voltaire**

Most world faith and wisdom traditions teach that the ultimate telos (goal) of humanity is oneness, or unity; yet it is often the territorialism created by differences in church dogma on this very subject that alienates. In setting out their stall, each religion creates in and out groups; those who believe and those who don't.

Religious rituals give us the warm glow of membership and affiliation; a sense of belonging that reaches deep in to our tribal nature, our need to belong to the group. This belonging to the group or herd is a very ancient instinct, dating back to early in our evolution. Belonging meant increased safety, the benefits of hunting together and the increased food source that resulted, opportunities for reproduction, protection during sleep, and information on potential dangers.

This instinct to belong is hardwired in to our psyches, and studies have shown that even the feeling of perceived exclusion, such as not being invited to lunch, or not included in a chat, activates some of the same neural pathways in the brain as physical pain. The discomfort acts like an internal electrical prod to steer us back into the safety of the herd.

Unfortunately, groups are defined by having a 'those that aren't included', or else everyone is in the group, and it isn't really a group. Oneness – the aim of so many religious and wisdom traditions – requires that we recognise this tribal tendency in ourselves, and consciously choose to be more than a collation of primal instincts; instead aspiring to become fully conscious, engaging, choosing and active participants in the raising of the collective consciousness of humanity through our daily living. Is it possible for us to consider unity more important than tribe?

Letting go of the religion we were brought up in can be a result of many things. Repetition can be the enemy of awe, so that familiar things begin to feel more like old hat than our favourite slippers. A move away from organised religion can be an act of alive religiosity, a move away from religion by rote, or an act of engaging with beliefs, of consciously and actively choosing what we believe and what we don't.

Such efforts demand that we care enough to consider our position on specific teachings, and reflect on whether or not they ring true for us. A lapse in religion can be a lapse into disengagement, a statement of anger against an institution, or a sign of increased commitment and continued searching for ultimate truth.

> '**People demand freedom of speech as a compensation for the freedom of thought which they seldom use.'**
> **– Søren Kierkegaard, Philosopher**

God of Our Skin Colour

It is probably fair to say that it is the anthropomorphic images of God – the angry, jealous or wrathful God – that have caused conflict, by humans, against humans. Over the centuries, tribes and countries have waged wars in the name of a God that has 'chosen' them. When faced with the unknowability of what is known variously as the Godhead, Brahman or the Tao, among many other names, we have a habit of transferring our own biases and preferences onto God as we know Him/Her/It. We give this entity our ego, our inner voice, our reasoning, our prejudices, and unconsciously even our skin colour. This increases His/Her/Its likeability for us considerably. Our tendency to like what we perceive as being like us is seen across many situations. We attribute similar attitudes and characteristics to people we vote for, or who belong to the same political party, as we attribute to ourselves. Job interviewers have been shown to be more likely to unconsciously bias their judgements about applicants according to the perceived similarity between themselves and the applicant. The same hair colour as your interviewer will help your application – just hope you don't remind them of their ex-partner.

In Sweden, the Evangelical Lutheran Church is rewriting liturgical language to encourage gender-neutral language when referring to God, to render God beyond human gender determinism. Perhaps such a move can reinstate the All that Is in Its rightful place far beyond the whims of humankind.

'As truly as God is our Father,
So truly is he our Mother.'

– Julian(a) of Norwich,
fourteenth-century Christian mystic

•••••••••••••••••• On Reflection ••••••••••••••••••

With the busyness of our lives, our spiritual beliefs can come very far down the list of things for our attention. Take the time here to become conscious again of where you are in your spiritual life – and how you got here.

What concepts of God or a higher power resonate with you, or do any? What do you consider sacred in the world? Has this changed over your lifetime?

Are there concepts which rile and irritate you, or make you feel different and distant from anyone with such a belief?

What do you consider to be the spiritual aspects or moments of your life?

Do you have spiritual experiences every day?

There is no need to try to challenge any answers which may come to you at this point. The aim is simply to bring to awareness our own understanding of our spiritual life, how we got here and the boundaries of our beliefs.

As we will see throughout these pages, our spiritual life is the inner dimension of ourselves that relates to things more than ourselves. In this way, it includes but transcends us, crossing our physical outline in relationship to something bigger than ourselves. It is self-transcendent in nature. It is at the same time both deeply interior and expansive.

For the believer, spirituality can be a relationship with God or other divinity; that from which we find a meaning and purpose to our lives; a value system; virtues to cultivate; and a complete system of living and dying.

But equally for those without any belief in a divinity, those of us who do not believe in a higher power can also find immense rewards in the self-transcendence of spirituality. It is, in fact, only by living in relation to that which is outside of ourselves, and greater than ourselves – be that our children, our work, a life of compassion, or becoming a better version of ourselves – that any of us can locate the meaning of our lives. Our relationship to the outer world places our existence on the map of things. It is in these aspects of connection that meaning can be found. In this lies our spiritual wellbeing.

Being SBNR can seem to offer the individual a new sense of experiential spirituality, access to feelings of wonder and an increased closeness to a higher power. Often those who classify themselves as SBNR say that they believe in 'something' but are not sure what it is. Others retain their faith in a Christian or other God but feel that they can now enjoy feelings of direct relationship with God that were lacking in religious celebrations, which for them felt tired and repetitious. It seems that for many, religion is full of humans, and spirituality, full of God.

There are many different ways to be SBNR. But for some, it can lack something in terms of tradition that can be passed on. The greatest appeal of being spiritual but not religious – the fact that it is personal and self-directed by nature – might also be its biggest weakness.

Without foundational teachings, being spiritual but not religious can create an experience of the esoteric that is unchallenged and unmediated, where we can act as our own judge and jury. It can be so deeply personal that it fails to offer the individual the benefits of shared experiences. The experience of present bliss that it provides – in a sunset, in nature, in art – while fulfilling, can be involuntary and fleeting; spiritual moments can feel accidental, rather than planned.

Ongoing spiritual development requires conscious and active engagement in its path, combined with a conscious choice to integrate it into every part of our living: our actions, our attitudes and our aspirations. The Seven-Day Soul offers us such a framework.

As we shall see, spirituality is crucial to the healthy functioning of society. Whether you hold traditional religious beliefs, or have developed your own framework for a spiritual life; and whether you have beliefs about a higher power or not, this book will help you explore how we can move ourselves forward in our role in developing a more compassionate society.

In the following conversations, two women speak

about their spiritual views. In the first, Beth explains her very earth-oriented spirituality, which might usually be described as Paganism or pantheism. In the second interview, Cathy describes the very common feeling of an evolving spiritual life in transition, a spiritual life where doubts and values can co-exist.

Beth's Story: The Spirit of the Earth

My own personal conception is that spirit infuses all things – animals, plants, even rocks and non-living things too. I experience the seasons as a reminder of a cosmic intelligence, beyond the control of humans. Huge and powerful, without them nothing would grow. To me, the earth is sacred. She is in charge, and we come along for the ride, for a short time. I recognise that the earth existed long before we came along – and that her challenges are mostly caused by humans. In my conscious awareness of this, I can attempt to act in a way that honours my relationship to the earth, and my debt to her.

Cathy's Story: Allowing Doubt – A Developing Spirituality

I was raised in a Catholic family, but I'm not really sure what I am. It's almost a pressure to call yourself something! I do believe in something, some kind of God, and I definitely want a Catholic funeral. I'm just not really into all the rest of it. I think you don't need to go to mass to be a good human being, a good and kind person.

The only thing that gets to me a bit is wondering if I have done the right thing for the kids. I do feel a bit guilty that they don't have what I had growing up. Faith gave you a sense of confidence. I hope that the children will grow up to be good people – but that's not the same as having a religion or believing in God. Of course, those two things are not exactly the same. I hadn't really thought of them as different until now . . . I might try to do something about that. The God part – I do think it's important. I'd like the kids to have faith, I'm not quite sure how I'd describe it to them. I don't want to tell them something I don't believe.

A Unifying Philosophy

Spirituality can offer us a life of meaning, a life lived in relationship to a larger context than the self. It provides an approach, an attitude and an overarching scaffold that holds up the minutiae of our daily life. It imbues everything with relevance, meaning and the possibility of understanding more deeply. Tasks become opportunities to live out our values, to grow personally and to play our part in the spiritual evolution of the world.

Dr James Fowler developed a model of the change that occurs in the development of faith of any kind. In modern conversation, we tend to separate faith from spirituality, associating faith with the belief in creeds and doctrines, and the latter with 'feeling' whatever we consider sacred. But in his research, Fowler took a much broader concept of faith when he collected the thoughts and beliefs of hundreds of people from aged four to eighty-eight, members of religious traditions and atheists alike.

In his theory of the stages of faith, Fowler took an all-encompassing understanding of the word 'faith', which he took to mean the universal quest of each of us for meaning and values in life. Faith here means our system of images, values and commitments that guide our life, religious and non-religious alike. Ultimate development, in Fowler's mind, is much more than simply holding the line, but an open, non-defensive, welcoming and inclusive attitude of universal connectedness. His stages of faith are described as:

Stage 0: Infancy – no spirituality

Stage 1: Intuitive-projective faith – egocentric stage

At this point the child is oblivious to the perspective of others.

Stage 2: Mythic-literal faith – conditioning stage

Here the child internalises teachings from adults and is particularly susceptible to social pressures.

Stage 3: Synthetic-conventional faith – conformist stage

The need to belong to the group takes precedence over individual needs, and the adolescent feels strong pressure to conform in order to solidify his or her social bonds.

(Note: It is perhaps religious beliefs at these early stages that cause most antagonism and are most criticised because the person has yet to internalise their spirituality. It has more to do with social membership with rigid beliefs which can cause feelings of 'us' versus 'others', and lacks the open, allowing and inclusive nature of later stages.)

Stage 4: Individuative-reflective faith – individual stage

With time, the individual may choose to go against the pull to belong to the group, and instead begin to think more individually and for him/herself.

Stage 5: Conjunctive faith – integration stage

Here, the individual begins to recognise a sort of collectiveness, a universality, and their equal place in the diversity.

Stage 6: Universalising faith – teaching and healing stage

Fowler thought it was only a very small number of people who reached this stage, where the person has no personal agenda, and a deep-seated sense of the inter-connectedness of all things. However, as these would be humble people and would tend to keep away from the limelight, Fowler said that it was difficult to estimate their numbers.

Fowler wrote that it was only a minority of people who ever make the transition from the tribal conformism of Stage 3 to the individuated thinking typical of Stage 4, and again, even fewer who grow from Stage 4 into Stage 5.

··················Checking In··················

Do certain individuals spring to mind as you read through the stages of faith? It could be tempting to take these stages of development as a way of judging others as, for example, stuck or conformist; but what does this tell us about ourselves? Even the spoken belief in the unity of all things can become a stick to beat others with – a spiritual high ground. Instead of judging others, it might be more useful to come back over and over again to our own learning and practise of compassion, allowing others to be with their own beliefs.

Do you have an agenda? What opinions might make you shout at the television? Noticing these times can be a great teacher in self-awareness and our habit of judging. It acts as a marker to our own boundaries – the points or values which we feel are non-negotiable. These points are like the tectonic plates of the earth's crust – almost unmoveable, but when they do move, they affect everything. Noticing these flashpoints helps us to wake up to our deeply held beliefs and values, which in turn helps us to step out of autopilot thinking.

The practise of noticing where we judge doesn't mean that we can never judge again – of course we need to make judgements throughout our day. But it can help us to see that we have set beliefs and ways of seeing the world that we all consider to be the 'right' way. We work hard to recruit others to our way of thinking.

Going back to the idea of working on ourselves rather than judging others requires us to see if it is possible to at least try to see the other person's point of view. What have they seen that you haven't? Would knowledge about where the other person lives, or the history of their country or family, help you to see through their eyes?

Postponing judgement is the first step to understanding. If we want peace or oneness to be more than a pipe dream, it starts with us.

Going by Fowler's model, spirituality that is opted into rather than fallen into may represent a maturing spiritual nature and a move towards the individuation of a person – the difference between opting in and being co-opted in. This 'opting in' can happen in organised religions and outside of them, in theistic and non-theistic spirituality.

'Credo' is a Latin word that is now translated and used in religious celebrations to mean 'I believe'. But according to some theologians, it was originally meant to mean, 'I engage with'.

Many people who struggle to believe in some

religious teachings would be more than willing to commit to engaging with them. To engage with involves a far lesser demand on the spiritual seeker – it opens up the journey. And engagement offers the potential of experiencing the divine, instead of simply talking about it in statements of creed and doctrine. It suggests a willingness to listen and consider in the company of doubt. It opens the door to questioning, and moves from professions of faith to allowing variations and alterations in belief within a person over time, and between individuals.

'Until faith becomes rejection, and rejection becomes belief, there will be no true Muslim.'
– Idries Shah, *The Way of the Sufi*

Whether people have turned away from organised religion because they hold the rational mind in highest value, or whether those who opt out of organised religion are in fact maturing in spirituality, spirituality has not gone away. The search, and perhaps the need, to make sense of the ultimate context in which we exist, cannot be dampened.

'The living spirit is eternally renewed and pursues its goal in manifold and inconceivable ways throughout the history of mankind. Measured

against it, the names and forms which men have given it mean little enough; they are only changing leaves and blossoms on the stem of the eternal tree.'
– Carl Jung, *Modern Man in Search of a Soul*

The idea that we need not only a personal relationship with God (as we know It), but also a more universal collective recognition, is what takes spirituality further than the personal realm. True spirituality transcends the self. It includes our inner life, but it also expands and connects our inner life with how we live our outer life.

'Truth is one; men call it by many names.'
– Hindu Vedas

The 'At One and the Same Time-ness' of Ourselves

For many years, science and spirituality have been seen as the enemy of each other, with spirituality retreating further from the frame every time science made a new discovery. But when we look at the discoveries of quantum physics – the physics of particles far smaller than the atom – we can begin to see some similarities between science and the more abstract ways of knowing God mentioned earlier.

Theoretical physicist J. Robert Oppenheimer (sometimes known as the father of the atomic bomb) wrote in 1953:

To what appear to be the simplest questions, we will tend to give either no answer or an answer which will at first sight be reminiscent more of a strange catechism than of straightforward affirmatives of physical science. If we ask, for instance, whether the position of an electron remains the same, we must say 'no'; if we ask whether the electron's position changes with time, we must say 'no'; if we ask if the electron is at rest, we must say 'no'; if we ask whether it is in motion, we must say 'no'. The Buddha has given such answers when interrogated as to the conditions of a man's self after his death; but they are not familiar answers for the tradition of seventeenth and eighteenth century science.

A particularly famous study in physics known as the 'double-slit experiment' has shown that light, which we normally think of as a wave travelling through space, can in fact be *both* a wave and, at the same time a particle. In trying to wrap our heads around this we might like to believe that the wave is actually then made up of lots and lots of particles, but this is not what is shown by the findings. Just as Oppenheimer's electron is neither resting nor moving, changing nor unchanging, light is at one and the same time a wave and a particle.

What does all of this have to do with us? Well, this 'at one and the same time' nature of reality has also been applied to human beings. Writing in the nineteenth century, philosopher Emile Durkheim described human beings as 'homo duplex' – two-layered humankind. The first layer, the 'will', was all about ourselves and our bodily needs. The second layer, the 'collective unconscious', keeps the first layer in check, making us look after the needs of others.

Durkheim believed that this second layer of the collective unconscious is developed from childhood through social bonds, and allows us to learn (at least sometimes) to prioritise the needs of our group or society over our own desires and wants. The strength of the collective unconscious depends on the strength of social bonds that each of us grows up with; where there is a strong sense of community ties, it will grow solid and robust. But where this kinship and sense of mutual connection is weak, a sort of lethargy that Durkheim called 'anomie' develops – what we could call a type of 'heart-lost-ness'.

There are many ways to try to understand our dual nature, the finite and the infinite aspect of ourselves. It can certainly be difficult to wrap our heads around these very mysterious concepts, which seem to fly in the face of how we experience the world. After all, something either is or isn't in our material world. But we don't all have to use the same language or metaphors as the scientists to speak about these things, but only to make sure that the conversations continue. The subject of spirituality in all its guises is a fascinating one, endlessly worth engaging with – to acknowledge it, investigate it, be with it, allow it, to give permission for the wondering and imaginative wandering to happen, so that we can better understand ourselves, our loved ones, our life and the lives of those we can love more.

'The final truths of religion are unknown, but a psychology that impedes understanding of the religious potentialities of man scarcely deserves to be called a logos of the human psyche at all.'
– Gordon W. Allport, psychologist

•••••••••••••• On Reflection ••••••••••••••

In developing our Seven-Day Soul we will be trying to develop ourselves, and also to live a life more connected to the whole. See if it is possible for you to identify which parts of your day turn mostly towards your own needs (which is not wrong) and which towards something greater than any one of us. While your daily tasks may not change much from day-to-day, your conversation and attitudes can change completely. Each of us needs to ask ourselves what we are building for the greater good. A village is not simply a collection of houses. A community is much more than a collection of people. Both require an inter-connectedness and inter-relating to exist. We must learn to be 'at one and the same time' with our inner spiritual self (the vertical life plane) and our outer self-transcendent self (the horizontal life plane). This can be our challenge – and our triumph.

4

The Seven Pillars

Our Daily To-do List

'The highest form of wisdom is kindness'
– The Talmud

Most of us are familiar with the feeling of being a passenger in life, carried along its path more by default than design. There are so many to-do lists, so many things we are supposed to be, have and achieve. Happily, developing our spiritual nature is not about adding yet another to-do to our list. It is a way of engaging in the same tasks, in a different way.

The traditional psychological approach to personal growth tends to involve an inward–outward direction of looking, and living: first the self, then the outside world. Acts of service come second to the development of the self. The Seven-Day Soul model entwines the psychological with the spiritual, partially inverting this approach so that we also develop ourselves through service to others. But what is service? Service means living a life that includes our rights, but prioritises our responsibility to the world. Service is an act of love. When we see our daily duties through the lens of service, everything we do becomes an opportunity to better the world, and in doing so, ourselves. It is an outward-in approach to living, where the world is our practise ground rather than background to our development.

An attitude of service imbues the most mundane tasks with meaning, helping us to become increasingly conscious of the impact we have on the world. We consciously choose to better the imprint we will leave as our legacy. Life becomes our training ground, where we are given the opportunity to develop ourselves, to sculpt our spiritual muscles, and develop the mental disciplines that make us increasingly outward-oriented.

As a way of introducing this idea, here's a simple exercise.

Cast your mind back over your day so far or, if it is early in the day, to yesterday. Who have you come into contact with? Loved ones, strangers, shopkeepers, shelf-stackers, radio or TV presenters, callers, social media posts, receptionists, fellow queue-ers, pedestrians, neighbours, other commuters, the voices of authors and journalists you have read. Then ask yourself these questions:

- ✳ Who are the people that I have impacted upon?

- ✳ What do I think that impact was?

- ✳ Are there things I would rather change?

- ✳ To whom have I been of service?

- ✳ Is there anything I would do differently, from a place of service?

End with a short gratitude for the learning received in this practise; a simple 'thank you' or 'giving thanks' is all that is needed.

Opportunities to be better versions of ourselves once lost, are lost forever – we can never get back those moments. But we can use them to remind ourselves of the life we want to lead, the values we want to live by, and the person we want to have been when it is all over.

Perhaps you want to be of service to your higher power, to a family member, or to the dynamic relationship that exists between all things. Whatever we choose, our efforts in service create the repetition of compassionate actions, which in turn rewires the brain to make it more likely that we will act more compassionately in the future.

It is within this fostering of an ethic of service that we grow and develop as individuals, always aware of our place in the wider society and culture. This growth contributes to the spiritual evolution of humankind, towards a higher level of cognitive functioning, one which is deepened by the connection that comes from spirituality, where we can see more clearly the interconnectedness of all things that is not readily visible to us as human beings. This development works towards what is described in different ways across faith traditions as enlightenment; putting on the mind of Christ; Nirvana; and life's purpose. By developing a life of service, we develop ourselves and all of society.

The conscious development of compassion is not a modest goal. Compassion not only creates joy, connection and empathy, it also saves lives, prevents emotional, sexual and physical abuse, stops suicides, protects children, feeds the poor, houses the lost, saves relationships, stops bullying, prevents war, and all of those other things that we can so easily forget to be shocked by – or believe fall outside of the remit of our own responsibility. These are not someone else's responsibility. Each of us is each other's 'someone else'.

In the final count, love is the be-all and end-all of the spiritual life. As such, it should be the first and last of everything we do. Kindness is one of the most common ways we speak about love, perhaps because we are too self-conscious to use the word 'love' itself.

Studies have shown that people tend to rate themselves above average in assessments on intelligence, attractiveness and driving skills. It may well be the same with acts of kindness, because of what is known as the self-enhancement bias. This unconscious tilt in our thinking makes us feel that we are somehow better than average. It buttresses our self-esteem and makes us feel good about ourselves. But it also means that we can over-generalise our own gloss, remembering our good deeds more easily than the deeds we would rather forget. Most of us would probably describe ourselves as being a good person – and we probably are. But there is always room for improvement. Love is a very big task.

What Love Asks of Us: The Two Life Planes of the Seven-Day Soul

Bringing spirituality in to our everyday lives requires that we attend to both our inner and outer life through the two life planes of spirituality.

Imagine these two life planes to be the vertical and horizontal axes on a graph.

The First Axis: The Un-earthed Life Plane

The vertical, or upright, axis is the first one. This includes the stilling, opening, centring inner practises of prayer, meditation, and/or contemplation.

In silence, or with the gentle inner voice of a mantra,

we remain in stillness, allowing thoughts to pass by, without trying to stop them. For those readers with a faith practise, the intention brought to this stillness might be of openness to the presence or voice of God, or to simply wait in patient receptiveness.

For those without a theistic viewpoint, the stillness embodies an attitude of open awareness to what is in each moment, watching the various moods and broods of the mind as they come and go.

Stillness nourishes us, calming the sense of rush that envelops us from the hurried brain, allowing us to re-centre and re-group when we are being pulled in various directions. As such, the practise of meditation is like the stake in the ground that supports the plant, buttressing it, allowing it to grow upwards to the sun as it should. The vertical life plane, then, is our still stake in the ground.

The Second Axis: The Earthbound Life Plane

The second axis is the horizontal plane, the very earth-bound human experience of lived time. On this axis are all our doings: the tasks, duties, and scurryings of everyday life.

Anyone who wants to live a more fully spiritual life must live on both of these axes, which form part of all spiritual traditions, allowing the poised stillness of the vertical upright axis to nourish and inform everything we do, think and say on the horizontal axis.

It is no coincidence that the vertical, upright axis appears to visually connect the cosmic vastness above us, be that God or the known universe, to the earth upon which we stand. Like lightning that wants to earth itself in the ground, love needs us to earth itself in life.

In our Western culture, we so often partition spirituality away into, at best, particular days or times of the week. But spirituality is about relationship, be that relationship to God, a higher power, others, life's meaning, or something beyond the physical body. The Hebrew word for 'holy' is 'kadash', which means 'other'. Spirituality is by its very nature a transcendence of the self and our visible outline. Just as every musical note finds its beauty in relationship to the notes around it, so too can each of us only fulfil our highest potential in a life lived in relationship to something outside of ourselves – ourselves and something more.

Contrary to how it is sometimes conceptualised, spirituality is not some dreamy state but an active, deliberate choice in how to live. Love's flowering may be beautiful, but it is firmly rooted in the 'dirt' of day-to-day living.

'One act of pure love in saving a life is greater than spending the whole of one's time in religious offerings to the Gods.'

– Buddhist Pali Canon

'Excellence is an art won by training and habituation. We do not act rightly because we have virtue or excellence, but rather have these because we have acted rightly. We are what we repeatedly do. Excellence, then, is not an act, but a habit'

– Aristotle

Improving Our Spiritual Fitness

When we want to improve our physical fitness, we make a conscious choice to increase exercise, by clearing a space for it in our schedule. We might go to a gym and get an assessment so that we can be given a programme that will gradually increase our fitness levels if we put in the work.

In developing our spiritual nature, we also have to make effortful demands on ourselves, to create the optimum environment for spiritual growth and awareness. Just like circuit training, we have to put in the 'reps'!

But what we will find is that we do not so much have to clear a window of time in our day for this pursuit, but slowly open our consciousness into fostering a way of being at all times.

This takes time, and is a learned behaviour that only becomes automatic through multiple repetitions, no different to the child learning how to safely cross the road, or to cover their mouth when they yawn.

This awareness of the moment clears a space for

us to become better versions of ourselves. Instead of the moments of time seeming to flow into one another seamlessly, each moment, each conversation, email, thought, or action becomes an opportunity to open up the potency of that moment – to see all of potentiality available to us in that moment.

In doing this, we give ourselves choice in how we respond to the world around us. This is the basis of any mindfulness practise and the goal of all spiritual teachings – to wake up to how we are living. Much like the pond-skater that stands lightly on the surface of a pond, never knowing the whole world of flora and wildlife that exists in the water below, most of us spend our time skating from urgency to emergency, the next thing to be done, the next fire to be put out. Evolving spiritually does not add anything to our schedule, but only opens up the opportunities for a better version of ourselves, already at our disposal should we choose to engage with them.

The Good Samaritan

In 1973, two psychologists at Princeton University set out to measure the effects of personality and context in how and when we do and don't help others. Their research was based on the famous parable of the Good Samaritan, in which a man who had been beaten and left for dead at the side of the road was ignored by a priest and a Levite, two religious people, but was saved by a Samaritan man who came from a section of Jewish society that was considered lowly and unclean. The Princeton researchers wondered when and in what circumstances any one of us might be the person who walks on by.

The researchers set up an experiment in which they recruited seminarians (individuals training for the priesthood) for a supposed study on religious education. They arranged the study to have a number of variations to allow them to vary the sense of hurriedness of the seminarians, and also the task they would be asked to do.

The seminarians were first called to one building, where they completed a personality assessment questionnaire, and questions about their motivations for studying for a religious life. The researchers divided their responses to this question into two categories – 'intrinsic motivations', such as 'I want to do good in the world' and 'extrinsic motivations', such as 'I want to go to heaven when I die'.

The seminarians were then instructed to go to a second building, where they were either told that they would have a talk on the parable of the Good Samaritan (in the hope that this would prompt thoughts of helpfulness) or where they would be asked to prepare a talk on seminary jobs (a more neutral task). Some were told that they had plenty of time, others that they were running late and needed to hurry, and a third group that they had a few minutes but should head on over anyway.

The research team had planted an actor masquerading as someone in need along the route to the second building. The man lay slumped in a doorway of an alley, moaning and coughing. The researchers observed the responses of the seminarians as they passed.

The results of the study showed that the sense of hurriedness had a major effect on helping, but there was less of a difference between those who had been told they were going to a talk on the Good Samaritan and those who hadn't. Their motivations for joining the religious life had little relevance either. Overall, 40 per cent offered some help to the victim. Where the sense of being rushed was low, 63 per cent helped, when people were on time, 45 per cent of seminarians helped, but when hurry was high, only 10 per cent helped. A few even stepped over the man.

The results suggest that thinking about ethics and norms does not mean that we will live by them. The speed of our lifestyle may dictate what we actually do. How many of us have spent a weekend at a retreat learning about what values we want to live by, but then crash-landed back in to 'real life' and all our habitual responses?

Today's pace of life is faster than ever before, and this often dictates how we react to the world around us. Context is far more relevant to how we behave than we give it credit for, no matter how good our intentions are. The experiment shows that we cannot leave our spiritual development to chance, or even to our best intentions, but must work consciously each day, actively priming ourselves to see everything we do as an opportunity to learn.

Aiming to build our self-compassion can be more useful than aiming to build self-esteem while we are learning. While self-esteem suggests an evaluation that requires us to see ourselves as better than average in whatever we do, self-compassion avoids the need to be anything more than someone who is trying, and gives us the heart to try again.

The Pillars of the Seven-Day Soul

The Seven-Day Soul is built on the daily practise of one of seven pillars, each of which helps us to develop our mind and soul in tandem towards fulfilling our personal potential.

The seven pillars are:

1. Generosity

2. Gratitude

3. Forgiveness

4. Patience

5. Awe

6. Humour

7. Stillness

When we repeatedly give our attention to these seven pillars, they become part of who we are, because what we do, we become. These pillars acknowledge the dynamic aspect of ourselves, our ability to grow and improve ourselves, our consciousness and that of all humanity, through persistent attention to our thoughts, attitudes and actions.

Bookend Your Day

Each day, select one of the seven pillars to give your attention to, making it your way of living that day. Change the order in which you work through the series, so that you do not find yourself applying the same pillar in the same situations each week. Let that pillar act as your lens through which you see the day's activities as opportunities, ripe with the chance to move you towards who you can be – a better version of who you already are.

As you wake, take a few moments to preview the things you need to do, the people you may meet and places you will go. Decide in that moment to live the day ahead through the lens of your chosen pillar.

Recognise and accept that your attention will be pulled elsewhere several times throughout your days, but as the days pass and you make this your way of living, you will very quickly notice that you remember your intention for that day more regularly.

At first, you might find that it is the times when you could have acted a certain way and didn't that come to mind fastest, after the fact, when it seems too late to do anything about it. But it is never too late, and that is all part of the growing. Every time we become aware of even a missed opportunity to have acted a different way, we make it more likely that we will remember the next time. In this way we strengthen the circuitry of the brain, which corresponds to mindful awareness and the value we want to act on. Each time this happens, we increase the likelihood of this virtue coming to mind again. It is all about the repetition and the next moment which brings with it another opportunity.

'Win the moment in front of your face.'
– Joe Schmidt, coach to the Irish rugby team

At the end of each day, take a few minutes to review it. Again, rather than trying to find time to do practise before collapsing into bed if that is what you normally do, you might choose to do it as you have a quiet cup of tea, as you brush your teeth, or undress for bed. For those who pray, it may become a part of your prayers or indeed your only prayer, for all acts of love are prayers. If you find that you are simply too tired to carry out your review at the very end of the day, try other times such as on your commute home, or while you exercise, or at mealtimes. It doesn't mean that you have finished applying your pillar for the day, but achieving this review is important, so you need to be honest about when you can realistically undertake it, thereby making it a practise that will last.

Journalling

Using a notepad or electronic device is a useful way to keep track of your practise. The time and effort it requires to write something down ensures your attention is secured for the duration of your writing, which again strengthens the corresponding neural networks in the brain. When it comes to the brain, whatever we pay attention to grows; fear and love are no different in this regard. Journalling, the act of writing, is a proven way to increase the likelihood of reaching our goals, whether they are career goals, weight loss goals, or spiritual goals.

Your daily journal entries should include:

* The date

* Your chosen pillar for the day

* Notes on opportunities taken and opportunities missed to practise the chosen pillar

✳ Gratitude for the opportunity to grow and flourish made as a prayer to God, your higher power, the universe, or simply the vast potential within you. For example:

'For this learning, thank you.'
'I give thanks.'
'For what I am and what I can be, I am grateful.'

The final step in diarying is to acknowledge that there are always opportunities that we have missed, or that have gone unnoticed. This step requires us in prayer or in intention to look towards the next day with our eyes continuously attuned to the needs of others, and opportunities for us to make our impact on the world.

It may be as simple as using one of the following phrases:

'Tomorrow I will be more (generous/patient etc).'

'Lord, let me be a channel of your (forgiveness) tomorrow.'

'Tomorrow, I will tune my eyes to the need for love in every minute of my day.'

'Tomorrow, I will love more.'

'Tomorrow, a little better.'

Some of the seven pillars may appeal to you more than others, or perhaps you feel that some are already your personal strong points. Others will be more of a challenge. Rotate each one throughout your week regardless.

Be aware that we all have blind spots. As we improve our conscious awareness of each of the pillars, it can be easy to become complacent, which can blind us to the potential to push our growth out to new heights. But being content where you are is not growth, it is simply treading water. The aim is to be moving, building on even the tiniest of growth that we have achieved. Again, self-compassion will be our friend here more than self-esteem. We can be grateful and even proud of any instances when we acted a little better than we might have before, even while knowing there is always more to be done.

If life is too full of physical or psychological challenge, it can feel like there is simply not enough mental energy available for spiritual growth. But remember that developing the Seven-Day Soul is not an add-on, but an add-in, to what we do. When life feels like a constant uphill trudge, or a repetitive and empty treadmill, building our spiritual selves gives meaning and purpose to the journey. It can actually lighten our psychological distress. It makes not what we do matter, as much as how we do it. It means that when it comes to the end of our time on earth, we will feel secure in the knowledge that we have made a worthwhile contribution, by playing our part in the evolution of humankind towards a kinder, more compassionate common mind. We will have lived a life of service.

These seven pillars should not be used as measuring sticks with which to judge others. Building the Seven-Day Soul is a private endeavour, where each of us works on ourselves and only ourselves, albeit for the benefit of everyone. If you find yourself 'measuring' someone else, notice that your attention has been grabbed from your inward focus, and use the opportunity to see if it is possible for you to bring your daily practise to bear on the moment. It is so easy to get lost in mental chit-chat about the accuracy or 'rightness' of our observations of other people, but that is not our job. Our task is to see if it is possible for us to exercise our daily practise of love in the available window of opportunity. Each pillar is a way of love, not leverage.

5

The Vertical Axis

Meditation: Our Still Stake in the Ground

'If every day you practice walking and sitting meditation and generate the energy of mindfulness and concentration and peace, you are a cell in the body of the new Buddha.'

– Thich Nhat Hanh

Meditation

In learning to live a more spiritual life, we need to first till the soil, to prepare the ground that will nurture the behaviours we want to grow. Learning to live deeply takes practise and time, and it is all too easy for good intentions to be forgotten in the hurriedness of life.

Most people hope to live a good life, a life with meaning. But growing our spiritual life takes effort and attention as well as good intentions. It requires that we actively nurture attitudes and ways of being that will inform our living, daily reorientating ourselves towards the spiritual skillset we want to develop. Living more deeply needs the sometimes dull, repetitive strokes of small acts of compassion, more than the fireworks of grand judgements and opinions.

Meditation forms the vertical life plane of the Seven-Day Soul – that still stake in the ground that supports us and prevents us from being pulled by our emotions. Whether you have theistic beliefs or your spirituality is more earth-or body-centred, in meditation we can all develop our sense of our still, sacred centre, our soul; our higher self, our authentic self or heart chakra. For some, this centre will be a connection to a higher power, something that transcends the physical boundaries of the body. For others, it is sacred in itself and requires nothing more.

Meditation is a general term used to describe the numerous methods of coming to stillness that have been taught worldwide for centuries. Stillness refers to both a physical stillness and an attentional stillness which we practise to slow the stream of thoughts that normally charge through our mind unchecked.

There are thousands of different forms of meditation, with differing foundational teachings, intentions and methods. Some involve the reading of sacred scripture, while others use a mantra or sacred word as a means to centre our awareness. Some aim to train our attention; others, all of our being. Some methods aim at stilling the flow of thoughts, and others at observing them, without trying to stop them, but only to know them more.

In some practises, this stilling of the mind is the end goal; in others it is a way of becoming more receptive to communication with the divine. Mysticism is the term used to describe more esoteric ways of interpreting the holy scriptures of world religions. These methods tend to be more experiential in that they can help us to 'know' our spiritual life rather than the more cerebral, language-based way of 'knowing about' the spiritual life that most of us have been taught.

These more abstract interpretations of the divine were often handed down from the teachings of men and women – known in the Christian tradition as the 'desert fathers' and 'desert mothers' – who removed themselves from normal society, and went into isolation to pray. But every tradition has its own version of mysticism, such as Sufism in Islam and Kabbalah in the Jewish tradition. Their deep, prolonged and often silent methods of prayer common to all of these traditions have come to be known as meditation and contemplation. Many of us in the West have been introduced to meditation through the rising popularity of mindfulness meditation which was adapted from the Buddhist tradition. Mindfulness in Buddhism is a fundamental teaching of the Eightfold Path of Enlightenment, the principle teachings of Theravada Buddhism.

The Eightfold Path to liberation and the end of suffering in Theravada Buddhism teaches us ways of living to aspire to:

* Right view

* Right intention

* Right speech

* Right conduct (action)

* Right livelihood

* Right effort

* Right mindfulness

* Right samadhi (meditative absorption)

The Sanskrit word for meditation is 'bhavana', which can be translated as 'mental culture'. So meditation is a way of cultivating the mind. In mindfulness we learn to observe the constant stream of consciousness that narrates and judges as we go through the day, often taking us back to the past or forward in to the future, rarely seeing reality as it is, without the judgements, emotions and stories added by the mind. Through the practise of mindful awareness, we can learn to observe our jumping 'monkey mind', and in observing it, we learn that if we can observe our thoughts, then we are not our thoughts. With practise, we can learn to access pure awareness, the space in which thought takes place that is larger, more still and untainted by our inner narrator.

During the late 1970s, Jon Kabat-Zinn, an American professor of medicine emeritus at the University of Massachusetts Medical School, saw the potential of mindfulness meditation as a way to ease the suffering of patients, non-patients and all of society. Already an expert in mind–body medicine, Kabat-Zinn saw the relevance of the teachings of mindfulness to all human suffering. After studying the teachings of Buddhist mindfulness practise, he developed the mindfulness-based stress reduction (MBSR) programme, an eight-week, group-based meditation training which he initially taught to people suffering with chronic pain, but which he later introduced to mixed patient groups. The practise and format offered the participants the kinship and support of the group, while at the same time avoiding an over-focus on any one type of pain or suffering within the group.

The programme involved once-weekly group meetings with daily home practise between sessions. The relatively high level of intensity of practise demanded of participants was deliberate and intended to ensure that participants really committed to the practise and valued it. It also ensured that the group achieved the repetition needed for real and measurable behavioural change and physiological change in the brain. But the reason mindfulness managed to make the leap that so many other ancient practises fail to make, was because the programme was tightly designed, with a detailed, prescribed structure which could be replicated in other research centres.

With little variation allowed, researchers could now run the MBSR programme in different locations and know that they were comparing like with like. With the development of functional MRI (fMRI) studies, as well as more traditional research methods, it was finally possible to build up the body of research needed to show that mindfulness meditation was indeed a useful tool in the treatment of many conditions and in the alleviation of suffering (albeit not the panacea for all ills that it is often thought to be). The ancient practise of meditation had finally become mainstream.

Despite its Buddhist roots, the MBSR programme was designed as a secular intervention so that it was appropriate for people of all faiths and none, and could be delivered in a clinical setting. But as we know, in its essence, mindfulness is a deeply spiritual practise, which is taught in various forms in most faith traditions.

In mindfulness, connecting with the breath is the most commonly used method of guiding awareness – we rest our attention on the breath, and return it to the motions of breathing when we notice that our mind has wandered. The breath is always with us, so it is a useful, portable entry point to observe the workings of the mind, no matter where we are or what we are doing.

Marion was a participant in one of my eight-week MBSR programmes. Her thoughts on the benefits and difficulties of mindfulness are something that most of us can relate to.

The first time I learned about mindfulness of the breath I found it a bit boring, to be honest, a bit repetitive and really hard to do. But after a while I realised just how much my mind looked for novelty all the time – it just couldn't stay on one thing for even a short amount of time! I was a bit annoyed with myself. I'm generally not too bad at concentrating – or so I thought – so I was really surprised by this. I think I also felt it was a bit pointless – who needs to be able to concentrate on the breath all the time?

But actually I noticed in my normal life – between sessions – that my mind hopped from one thing to another all the time. It was shocking, to be honest! I also noticed that I was breathing – just that simple fact, that I had never noticed before. And then I began to notice other people breathing, and it dawned on me that without that tiny movement of the chest none of us would be here. It's, like, so important! In a way we just take breath for granted, but it's literally the difference between life and death. I also began to notice my kids' breath and how beautiful it is. I sometimes just watch them breathing when they are sleeping or even talking.

It has become something I really notice now, so important and valuable and yet we just ignore it most of the time. Meditation really has opened my eyes to it.

This renewed appreciation expressed in Marion's experience of meditation is a beautiful description of its gifts: to awaken deeply to the preciousness of life as a result of learning to open out each moment, as if unwrapping a present someone has given to us.

Across the world meditation traditions, various mantras, mandalas and sacred words can be used in the same way the breath is in mindfulness: as a place to rest our awareness. In the Christian tradition's Centring Prayer the Aramaic word 'maranatha' is often used, meaning 'come, Lord', indicating the intention of the meditation as a means to be open to God's presence within.

No matter what tradition we come to meditation through, we can choose any word that is personally meaningful, as long as it doesn't bring up distracting imagery or emotion which might pull us away from our intention to openness. And whether we practise meditation as a religious or non-religious way to learn to live more deeply, we should not try to aim at a particular outcome or expectation for our sitting. We are not trying to achieve psychological insights nor spiritual experiences nor epiphanies – no matter how exciting they might sound! The purpose is simply to sit in stillness as best we can that day, without comparing it to another day or mentally grading how well we are doing. For those with religious beliefs, this stillness becomes meaningful in its intention to be open to God or other divinity; to become still enough to hear. But for all of us, sitting in stillness opens out each moment into something far beyond the limitations of time.

The Seduction of Our Attention by Emotion

Sufism, the mystical aspect of Islam, warns against the attraction for the beginner meditator in getting swept away by the imagination or feelings of bliss. In a collection of stories called Tales of the Dervishes, spiritual writer Idries Shah recounts the story of a young man who is guided to a place where the dervish opens the earth and instructs the young man to descend and to collect a plain candlestick of iron.

As he descends, the young man is ecstatic to see countless jewels and treasures, which he quickly gathers. He also sees the iron candlestick, takes it and returns to the surface of the earth, where suddenly the treasures disappear from his arms, including the candlestick, and the dervish is gone. The candlestick turns out to be magical and can give him all he wishes, but is lost to the man due to his greed.

The story is a metaphor for the temptation to be

enticed by the lovely feelings we can sometimes experience in meditation. When this occurs, we miss the magic of the seemingly plain candlestick; we confuse the blissful feelings for the gift of unity and awareness itself.

When feelings of bliss or being overcome with positive emotion do come we should not try to 'keep' them, or get caught up in the visual imaginations that sometimes come with them, but simply allow them to come and go in their own time, constantly reorienting ourselves towards our breath or word.

Prayer and the Seven-Day Soul

For me, sitting in meditation became a prayer simply by making the sign of the cross at the beginning and end of my practise. This became especially meaningful to me when I learned to see the cross as the interconnection of the horizontal plane on which we live our lives, and the vertical plane which connects us to God, or the infinite.

Many of us have been raised on the notion of spoken prayer as the only means to pray. But the teachings of so many world traditions reveal that everything we do can be our prayer. When we understand that spirituality is about living, not just reciting, all our loving actions, right deeds, thoughts and words become our prayers.

Sitting in meditation practise is one way to pray, even when we do not speak or perform any rituals, such as blessing ourselves. The very act of sitting in stillness and attending to silence is a metaphysical kind of prayer, if that is what we intend it to be.

Whether we come to meditation with religious beliefs or not, it is a way of learning to see reality in a different way, a recognition that there exists more than the visible world we can see. The purpose of meditation is to inform the way we live our lives, so that we begin to bring that sense of being firmly rooted in stillness to all our judgements, conversations and tasks. Meditation changes the 'how' rather than the 'what' of our living.

As we will see in later chapters, daily repetitions will change the neural landscape in our brain, but the vertical life plane is not mere brain-training for concentration. It is about being pulled towards love like a compass needle finds its north. Meditation helps us to be present enough to notice opportunities for kindness, and to achieve a level of self-awareness to be able to choose how we respond when our buttons are pushed.

Learning in Reflection

Bring your attention to a recent time when you said something you regret. See if it is possible to rewind back to the moment between when you were still in control and the moment you lost that control – perhaps something in particular was said or done that pushed you over the line.

At what point in the conversation were you still speaking fairly and respectfully? Can you remember what it was that tipped you over the line between responding and reacting? What emotion was present in the moment? Perhaps a sense of injustice or being treated unfairly, or not being listened to? A feeling of hurt, envy, anger, frustration, tiredness, stress or even too many voices or environmental noise that you just couldn't cope with?

What might have been a better, but *realistic* alternative way to respond? Chances are you would not have been able to respond with absolute sweetness and perhaps it would not have been appropriate anyway. But perhaps there were some realistic alternatives that were available to you. Could you have said, 'I need to move away, we'll talk later when I'm calmer,' or 'I'm exhausted, I can't talk about this now,' or could you have said to a partner, 'Can you take over with the kids while I calm down?'

Sometimes simply admitting that you are tired and ratty is enough to diffuse the explosiveness of a situation. It is not an excuse, but is a moment of self-awareness that can ease tensions and open up options of ways to respond. See if it is possible for you to name your emotion(s) when you feel yourself being pulled. Introducing this honesty and having the presence in the moment to become aware is what we mean by living deeply – not darting across the pond surface like the pond-skater, but diving in to see what is below the surface. What can appear to be anger on the surface may actually be fear, envy, tiredness, hunger or stress. In diving into the moment, we open it up to our awareness so that we can act with more conscious choice, rather than by the automatic habits of a lifetime.

Developing this kind of mindful awareness promotes kindness, self-and other-compassion, and spiritual growth. The true nature of spirituality is found in the nitty-gritty of life – not rarefied or exalted, but at our disposal in responding to life's everyday, ordinary challenges.

A Seven-Day Meditation Practise: Connecting to the Universal and Eternal

Find a place where you can sit or lie where you will not be disturbed. This could be the floor, at your desk, in a favourite armchair or in your car, perhaps before going to the office, a meeting or bringing the kids to school.

Traditions vary in the length of time demanded for daily practise but ten minutes is an achievable length, that allows your mind time to settle but which is also a realistic starting point. Although we can also do one-, two- or three-minute meditations as a type of top-up during the day, it usually takes some time to settle the racing mind. So aim to begin with a minimum of ten minutes every morning, gradually building up to twenty minutes a day and more if you wish. At first, finding time to practise will certainly take some effort.

Depending on how busy your schedule is, you might choose to wake earlier – but having something light to eat before your sitting will ensure that you are not hungry and that your mind has energy to work with. Other people have told me they leave home and pull in somewhere on the route to work as it is the only place they won't be disturbed. That's fine too (but never listen to meditation CDs while driving, for obvious reasons).

Try to look upon your meditation as a sort of 'spiritual newsfeed', that much like the other type of newsfeed sends you updates and reminders throughout your day – this one about how you want to live your day. It is so easy for us to have good intentions but then get washed along by the tide of busyness and doing, just like the seminarians in the Good Samaritan experiment. Your meditation will become your constant reorientation to the values that you want to infuse your living, so that you live the life you intend to live. You live the day of your choosing.

Set an alarm on your phone or clock, but try to plan a gentle tone to let you know the time has elapsed, rather than one which jars with the stillness.

For your sitting, you can put a blanket over yourself if needed, but don't allow yourself to become too cosy or warm as this only invites sleep. Similarly, if you choose to do your meditation lying down, be aware of the associations with sleep and change to a different place if you need to. However, if you find that you fall asleep regularly and quickly during most daytime meditation sessions, you may be chronically sleep deprived, and getting more sleep might need to be your first priority.

Allow your eyes to close, or if this doesn't feel comfortable for you, allow your eye gaze to fall to just a few feet in front of you on the floor. Your chin should be slightly tucked in so that your neck is neither over- nor under-extended. Your legs should be uncrossed, with the soles of both feet (or shoes) on the ground. If you struggle with drowsiness during the sitting, try very slowly changing to a different position, perhaps sitting in a more upright position away from the back of the chair but avoid bringing any rigidity into the body. Sitting away from the back of the chair is a useful way to both keep us awake but also to get that sense of paying attention rather than drifting off, which we are trying to achieve.

You can choose to use your breath as the place you will rest your attention, or alternatively choose a sacred word to be repeated throughout the practise. However, try not to get pulled into the mind's tendency to tell a story about the word – it is simply meant as an anchor to rest your awareness on, and a place to come back to over and over and over again, whenever you find that your mind has wandered. Try not to get frustrated or irritated by the mind's tendency to wander; simply use the wandering as another chance to become aware of these tendencies and, without judgement, bring your breath or sacred word to mind once more.

You should not say the word aloud, nor mouth it quietly, but instead say it silently with your inner voice, methodically and repeatedly, throughout the practise. If you choose to rest your awareness on the breath, let go of any notions of the correct way to breathe, and try instead to simply accompany your breath as you find it, without trying to change it in any way.

The purpose of your meditation is to bring your gaze inwards towards that part of you that is still. But no matter what terminology each of us uses to understand this aspect of ourselves, our aim is to become so familiar with it that it adds a new dimension to everything we do, acting like subtitles on the screen of our vision, telling us what exists beyond the bandwidth of consciousness we habitually use. That somehow we are connected to a great universal stillness that surpasses the cluttered view of the world as we see it.

You might also like to choose a mantra such as truth, thanks or love for your meditation, but do not plan how you will utilise that concept in your day. Allow it to remain a sound vocalised by your inner voice.

When your meditation has ended, and before you open your eyes, you might want to mentally go through your day and see if there will be immediately obvious opportunities to practise your chosen spiritual lesson – this could be as simple as a lane of traffic where you repeatedly find yourself swearing at other drivers, or someone in the office who irritates you. There will of course be many other opportunities for practise that will arrive unannounced in your day.

Letting Go of Judgement in Meditation

With meditation, it is always tempting in the early stages of our practise to assess how we are doing, as is our human tendency in any new activity that we take up. The beauty of meditation, however, is that such self-judgement is not only unnecessary, it is to be avoided. The simple act of doing the practise with the intention of connecting to your still centre is what is important. There is no such thing as a 'good' or 'bad' practise or prayer. Any judgements are just more thoughts. Allow them to pass by, not trying to stop them, nor being tempted to jump into any inner conversation.

Remember that the more you try to stop your thoughts, the more you are adding to them. 'I just want to stop thinking' is a thought in the same way that 'Oh good, my thoughts are slowing down' is also just a thought. Let go of these types of striving by allowing thoughts to arrive and pass by, and return your awareness to your breath or word.

Try to do your practise where there is not too much noise. If this is not possible, use sound as another opportunity to notice how our attention is drawn to the novelty of the sounds around us. We can either choose to gently guide our attention back to our breath or word or alternatively, to give that sound our fullest awareness. In doing so, we notice the notes within the sound, the tiniest of silences between the notes and the stories our mind creates around the most mundane of sounds, such as, 'that's a car slowing down at the traffic lights outside', 'that's a truck reversing', 'that's a very young baby's cry', and so on. Rarely, if ever, do we attend to sound just as it is, in its purity. The same is also true of how we see and interpret all of reality.

A meditation on sound also helps us to realise that just as some sounds come and go, and others repeat themselves over and over again, our thoughts also come and go, while others hang around inside our mind, becoming regular and often unwelcome visitors. A sounds and thoughts meditation can also be a useful way to open up the sacredness of things we take for granted – such as the soundscape around us – and become a beautiful addition to our practise. Overall, our meditation on a mantra, sacred word or breath will be the mainstay of our practise. But opening up our awareness to the wider lens of the sounds around us can be really useful in teaching us the ability to switch between lenses on the world – to be able to see the woods *and* the trees.

'For lack of attention, a thousand forms of loveliness elude us every day.'

– Evelyn Underhill

During your practise you might experience tearfulness, joy and other shows of emotion. These are emotions which have not been previously released coming to the surface. Don't be tempted to stop them. Allow tears or other emotions to come, without any attempt to analyse or fix them.

Seven-Day Meditation Summary

Find a place where you can sit or lie undisturbed.

1. Start with a minimum of a ten-minute practise, setting a gentle alarm accordingly.

2. Be gentle with your body in holding your posture, but ensure it is not so comfortable that it invites sleep or cuts off your circulation.

3. Choose your sacred word to rest your awareness on, and repeat it in your mind without speaking it aloud. Alternatively, choose your breath as the stake in the ground for your awareness.

4. Your intention is not performance but to connect with the still centre within, what

others might call your heart chakra, your soul, or being present to the actions of God within.

5. Repeat your mantra throughout the meditation, or alternatively follow the movements of your breath without trying to change it in any way.

6. When you notice that your mind has wandered, bring it back to your word or breath. This you may do thousands of times; no matter, do it again.

7. Be gentle with yourself. Let go of striving; this is a place of safety, and acceptance of you as you come.

·················On Reflection·················

Pause from thought

If the only prayer we ever say is 'thank you', then this will be enough.

6

Do We End at Our Epidermis?

Exploring the Mystic Line

'Draw if thou canst the mystic line
Severing rightly His from thine
Which is human, which divine'

– Emerson

Over the last century, spirituality has gradually disappeared from public discourse, and has come to be considered a purely personal matter. We have become spiritually shy. Outside of our intimate circles of loved ones, most of us will resist speaking in the language of spirit – we will speak of someone feeling 'down' but not 'empty', 'depressed' but not 'lost'; and we will talk about our 'goals' but not our 'yearnings'. As a society, we have placed increasing value on the rational mind as the sole arbiter of being and experience, at a cost to our wellbeing.

When teachings on virtues, meaning, the transcendent

and the sacred are set aside, we are forced to find happiness in the remaining physical and mental realms. Happiness becomes an end in itself instead of a by-product of meaning. We confuse happiness with fulfilment: one a pleasure, the other a lasting contentment.

The difference between these two has become a hot topic in psychology and wellbeing research. Irish philosopher Dr Stephen Costello differentiates three types of happiness and maps them neatly on to the three dimensions of humanity: pleasure as a happiness of the body; happiness as we refer to it, a psychological happiness; and joy, a spiritual happiness. Increasingly, research in the area points towards purpose and meaning as the keys to this deeper, spiritual joy – the fulfilment that Aristotle called 'eudaimonia'.

While spirituality is deeply personal, it is not altogether a private matter. Its ends – love, purpose and meaning – are the result of spiritual needs from deep within our core, in an act of reaching out beyond the boundaries of our skin to find our place within the world. Love, purpose and meaning are by nature self-transcendent. They show us that it is in service of others and the world, rather than the self, that we find the happiness we are all searching for; a life lived with responsibility as well as rights.

If we want to reintegrate spirituality back in to our collective mental map of how we view our humanness, we need to begin by making conscious the mental maps we currently live by. Only when we become aware of them can we judge them to be useful or outmoded, helpful or unhelpful.

Without our knowing, each of us has already internalised many unconscious mental maps of how we experience the world, and these in turn affect how we relate to it. These mental metaphors help us navigate our way in life, to understand abstract concepts and discuss them with others in terms we can all relate to.

In the West, we imagine time to be an arrow that moves from left to right, but in China, the arrow of time moves from right to left, reflecting the fact that we imagine time to move the way we read text. Success is imagined as being up, as are good things. We say 'things are looking up' and when feeling low, we do something to 'cheer ourselves up'. If things are really positive we 'scale the heights'. Ideas are often seen as food: 'food for thought', 'half-baked ideas' and 'an insatiable curiosity'. Arguments are commonly imagined as war, giving rise to phrases such as 'winning an argument', 'attacking weak points right on target' and 'gaining ground' against the opponent 'in the firing line'. We have winning 'in our sights'.

These mental maps particularly help us to understand abstract notions such as ideas, love, happiness, success and so on, and in doing so they affect our daily reality. How much different the world might be if we saw an argument to be, for example, a dance, where each party needed to 'fall into step' with each other, or 'find their rhythm', realising 'it takes two to tango'.

It would be tempting to think that these metaphors come after the event; that they come into language to describe what already happens. Psychological research shows that in fact these concepts are handed down to us unconsciously from a very early age and affect how we behave. We try to win the argument because we see it as war.

Much the same can be said about how we conceptualise the spiritual dimension of ourselves. Those brought up in the Christian tradition will probably have grown up with an image of the soul as some type of cloud-like light at our centre that rises out of the body at death. But this is just a metaphor, used to more easily illuminate a concept – it does not provide an essential view of what the soul is. If, in adulthood, these images of a light or cloud become unacceptable to us, we may let go of belief in the spiritual aspect of ourselves instead of the metaphor. Rarely, if ever, was soul described to us as a path, a way, or a disposition (as suggested in the Tao), or way of life. Or as C.S. Lewis wrote, 'We do not have a soul. We are a soul.'

Would we treat our bodies in a different way if we considered them part and parcel of the soul? Would we stop attending to the body in the gym, the mind in education, and the soul in the church or synagogue once a week, and instead see our spiritual dimension as a way of living in our mind and body?

Where Is the Eternal in You?

There are as many ways of visualising your spiritual self as there are ways to be spiritual. There is no one way that is more 'correct' than another, but the mental images that we use affect how we see ourselves in the world. If you were to take a pen and paper right now and draw your spirit, where would you put it? Most of us rarely bring to conscious awareness 'where' we might put our soul or spirit in our map of ourselves, but just like our other mental maps, it has a lasting impact on how we live out our spiritual life and whether or not we fully inhabit our Seven-Day Soul.

Some of us will place our soul as the outer circle of three concentric circles, with the inner two circles representing the mind and body. Placing the soul as the outer ring represents the spirit as holding the other two dimensions of ourselves. In this model, all physical and mental events occur within the all-encompassing outer circle of spirit.

Others might label the inner circle as being their soul or spirit – the core of themselves, perhaps radiating outwards to the other two rings, or else as a stand-alone core of self. This would mean that a person's spiritual dimension has little bearing on their physical and mental lives but is something they either forget about, or visit in times of prayer or spiritual practise. It may represent something within them that is smaller than the other two dimensions of themselves, or a solid root system, unperturbed by the winds of physical and mental challenges.

Maybe you would draw your sense of self like a pie chart – where spirit and physical body and mind are each different slices, and perhaps there are many other slices in the pie. You might draw your roles as a parent or daughter, your career, and so on. This would suggest that you view your spiritual life as something separate, albeit perhaps very special or sacred, from the other parts of you.

Others, while also holding the belief that the human being is made of the three layers of mind, body and spirit, may view each layer as separate from each other or as a hierarchy with the physical, psychological or spiritual at the apex, depending on which level they consider to be the most important.

'The human personality, at its further limits, opens into the spiritual realm. Speaking metaphorically, one might say that the human personality is a river that, if navigated to its end, opens into the ocean of the mystic realm.'

– David N. Elkins

The Noetic Core

Viktor Frankl was a Viennese psychiatrist who was imprisoned in Auschwitz and other camps during the Second World War. Frankl, who we will return to at a later stage, lost almost every member of his family in the Holocaust, including his wife, mother and father.

During his detention, Frankl became interested in what allowed some prisoners to cling to hope for the future, while others passively waited for death or threw themselves against the electrified barbed wire fencing. Although a deeply religious man himself, Frankl wrote about spirituality as being about our existence in this life, and our responsibility to fulfil the meaning of our lives.

Frankl saw spirituality as a pull, drawing us to be responsible for who we are. He viewed the human being as being like a three-dimensional cylinder, with three concentric rings of mind, body and spirit and three horizontal layers representing the unconscious, pre-conscious and the conscious. Because for Frankl our spiritual core runs through all the layers of us, from conscious to unconscious, in body and mind, then some disorders that we would normally describe as psychological or physical could actually be coming from the spiritual part of us, but are showing up as psychological or physical ailments.

Frankl estimated that up to 40 per cent of psychological illnesses are actually calls of the spirit to force us to listen to our human need for meaning in our lives. He used the Greek word 'noos' to describe this spiritual part of us, but he did not intend it to mean spiritual in any religious sense. In using the word 'noos', he was referring to a higher aspect of the human person, the dimension of ourselves that understands what is true or real – what could be called our intuitive intelligence. Our noetic needs, then, coming from this part of us, are our need for values and meaning.

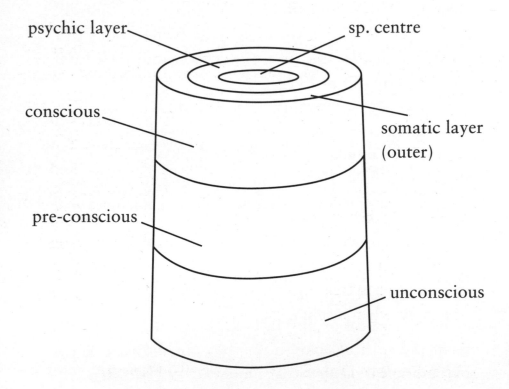

psychic layer

sp. centre

conscious

somatic layer (outer)

pre-conscious

unconscious

Frankl's 3-D cylinder metaphor of the human being.

While the difference between these models of where we might place the soul might seem overly academic, each of us carries through life such a mental model of our make-up; a way of visualising ourselves. These images of humanity are held in the collective psyche of every nation, guiding whole generations in their actions; parents raise their children, medics treat their patients, and teachers teach, according to the mental map of their era.

If that model is two-dimensional and features only the layers of body and mind, then what we include in a child's education, how we value green spaces in our town planning, what we look for in a partner, where we look for answers when times are tough, how we write our employment legislation, or how we explain the patient who doesn't recover despite successful treatment, are all limited to these two parameters. But where we have a model of ourselves as being constituted of mind, body and spirit, where each layer permeates the others, then we have another way of understanding and new pathways to explore in the search for healing in society and in ourselves. The doctor will remember the noos when treating the body, the teacher will engage the spirit when teaching the child.

The Seven-Day Soul Is W-holy Human

Spirit's greatest characteristic is its animating thoroughness – its ability to transcend personal boundaries and to energise and activate *everything we do* – not just the traditionally spiritual parts. It moves from internal to external in ever-increasing circles, connecting us with our loved ones, the wider world, the environment and, for some of us, the transcendent.

We might call spirit the ghost in the machine, the breath of life, the Holy Spirit or our true north. No matter how we know it, we need to build ourselves ways to integrate spirit into the pots and pans of our lives, so that what we gain in our meditation practise is fully brought to bear in the minutiae of our day. When we shift our tired perception, spirit comes pouring through into the second, horizontal plane of everyday living, and all our life becomes our pilgrimage.

• • • • • • • • • • • • • • • On Reflection • • • • • • • • • • • • • • • •

The following Hindu Upaniṣad is a call to each of us to discover the highest version of ourselves.

Asato ma sad gamaya
From unreal lead me to real
Tamaso ma jyotir gamaya
From darkness lead me to light
Mrtyor ma anrtam gamaya
From death lead me to immortality

Brhadaranyaka Upaniṣad 3:8

7

Everyday Epiphanies
Limbering Up for Life

'So many tangles in life are ultimately hopeless that we have no appropriate sword other than laughter'
– Gordon W. Allpoet

Have you ever noticed how particular songs can change your mood? How one will evoke a sense of sadness, while another will make you feel romantic, playful, or motivate you to run faster if you're listening while jogging? Building a values-focused day is a way of actively choosing to set the soundtrack of your day – to decide that you are going to see the epiphanies already present to you, to open your eyes to the beauty that stretches itself on the carpet of your day, unperturbed by your busyness. Unless this is something that comes naturally to you, you will need to make a conscious decision to move into this perspective, over and over again, until such time as it becomes simply how things are to you.

What you are likely to find is that this way of seeing quickly becomes so rewarding that you wouldn't have it any other way. It just becomes a pleasure, your chosen way of seeing. That's not to say that life will be a continuous stream of bliss – suffering is a part of life. But even suffering will connect you to that sense of something greater, the web of life and our responsibility to evolve.

During the practises of prayer and meditation, it can be tempting to hope for spiritual breakthroughs and moments of clarity, and it is disappointing when they don't happen for us, or seem few and far between. It can certainly feel like waiting for Godot.

But the practise of prayerful meditation in essence teaches us not to hope for such experiences, but to keep our thoughts firmly on the effort of emptying ourselves so that we may pay more attention. Learning to be present enough to really listen and to really see permits spirituality to come into every part of our day, to see that epiphanies surround us – if we would just take the time to look.

You can use the few moments after your morning meditation to set your spiritual soundtrack. Most of us will have a mental run-through of the day as we get up and get dressed anyway – what we need to wear, bring, whether or not we need a coat, who we need to call, and so on. If we wanted to remember to bring some clothes to the dry-cleaner's we might write it down at the top of that day's page in our diary, we might set a reminder on our phone, or stick a note to ourselves on the fridge door or the dashboard of the car. We will do everything we can think of to make sure we remember to bring those clothes to where they need to be. We need to do the same with remembering to see spiritually. We need to plan it into our day, and then give ourselves timely reminders throughout the day that this is something we want to do today.

Spirituality sometimes feels like such an abstract, woolly concept that sticking to our good intentions can be difficult. Unlike a goal-based approach to a pursuit, when we live spiritually, the goal is not an end result, but to live the journey well. It is the values that guide our movement through life that define us at the end of it.

The seven pillars of the Seven-Day Soul are your memos to yourself. Each one will act as your column of strength throughout that day. It should travel everywhere with you, be as much a part of you as your spine, helping you to stay upright when it is tempting to collapse into the easy path. Let it inspire you, energise you, change you. Let yourself really feel it as your spine beneath your skin.

In challenging situations, connecting and grounding to your pillar can inspire the next thing that comes out of your mouth, your next action. Do as you would with any personal goal – write it down in your diary, write it on a sticky note in your bathroom or kitchen where you will see it regularly, place a reminder in your wallet. As you will use the same seven pillars over and over each week, it is helpful to have each one written on a small laminated card that you can place in your pocket or wallet, or clip to the top of your diary page, to act as your constant reorientation to your spiritual living.

Make everything you do be your prayer, or your gift to the world. No matter what you need to do in your day, there will be countless opportunities to practise your Seven-Day pillar. Remember that there is nothing to be added to your to-do list, but only a different way of seeing what is already here.

At first it can be quite difficult to remember to switch into a more spiritual way of seeing things, and to stay connected to your loving lens on the world. We get pulled back into the dualistic lens over and over again, the sense of 'me' and everything that is not me.

But with repetition, the moments you remember to see through the lens of love will become more frequent, until those moments that started out as 'dots' throughout the day begin to string themselves together into dashes, more continuous periods of choosing to act with love. Our aim is make this our only way of living, unseparated from our intellect, so that there is no difference between the judgements of the rational mind and the intuitive mind, and all that is loving becomes the logical answer.

Spirituality of the Body

Despite our growing knowledge about what we should and shouldn't eat and the increasingly prevalent weight loss industry, it isn't often that we take a spiritual lens to our bodies. The body seems to respond to our dietary manipulations and various efforts to get ourselves moving, so it can be tempting to treat our body much like potters' clay, malleable to our needs. Coming to see our bodies as the most important facets of existence, the very essence of being, requires a renewed appreciation in our vision. Science so far has taught us that we are made of mostly carbon and oxygen, and these two, mixed with nitrogen, calcium and phosphorus, make up over 99 per cent of the human body. But why is carbon so fundamental to our existence?

Scientists believe that it is the carbon atom's stable nature that is responsible for its prevalence in nature. Carbon doesn't easily explode or disintegrate even under water, and can bond with more other atoms than most. Its stability is due to the fact that the electrons inside the carbon atom move in tight rings around its nucleus, and it is this closeness to the nucleus that makes it a very strong, stable atom.

As with other atoms, when scientists look more closely at the workings of the carbon atom they find it to be made up mostly of space. Here we come back to the mystery of life, the ghost in the machine, the non-material essence that animates everything, which makes the electrons move around the nucleus and build bonds with other atoms. This is the living field of your body, the miniature universe within, that simultaneously echoes the vastness of the universe that surrounds us. This is the very heart of the mystery of life: we cannot make life without using existing life.

A Reflection on the Body

Fearlessly and Wonderfully Made

Throughout the day, whether in the shower, while reading, playing sport, at the PC, walking from the car to your work, or wherever you might be, take just a few moments to give your attention to the mystery of life in your body. You can choose to close your eyes to be with the whole of your body or a chosen body part. Simply notice that part of the body, what it does for you and the innate intelligence contained within its cells to carry out their function day after day, far below your conscious awareness. When we appreciate the mystery of that which animates the electrons, neutrons and all particles of every atom of ourselves and all things, then we begin to knit ourselves back in to the web of life.

See if it is possible to bring gratitude to your body, perhaps patience with those parts of your body that do not work as you would like them to or as well as they used to. You might like to consider some of these incredible facts about the human body and rest in awe of the truth that you are fearlessly and wonderfully made:

* Your body contains approximately 96,000 kilometres of blood vessels.

* There are 2.5 trillion blood cells in your body at any one moment, and each red blood cell can circumnavigate the whole body in less than twenty seconds.

* Electrical messages travel through your nerves at a speed of approximately 400km per hour.

* The small intestine crammed into your body is approximately 23 feet long.

* The eye captures an image of what it sees upside down. This image is then made upright by the brain. (This is a wonderful reminder that we are always seeing the world through the filters of the human senses.)

* Most people have three types of receptors to see colour. However, some people are born with four and even five types of receptors,

allowing them to see more of what is really there, beyond the bandwidth of normal perception.

✴ The human body emits light called bioluminescence, which is too weak for the human eye to perceive. While not everyone is at home with the idea of human auras, it is this bioluminescence that specialised cameras have attempted to capture to try to assess the emotions and health of the body in aura reading. Of course the existence of bioluminescence doesn't necessarily mean that it changes immediately or at all as our moods fluctuate, or that it in any way reflects our state of health. But it does remind us that there is more to the world than our eyes can see and that in itself is a precious lesson.

I would also like to share with you something that, for me personally, has become a very special way to appreciate the wonder of the human body.

In the Buddhist tradition, a temple bell is sometimes used as a reminder to come home to one's true self. Every time the monks hear the sound of the bell, they stop what they are doing for a moment and bring their attention back to the breath and their true nature. We can all adopt this practise, using reminders of any kind – closing a door, finishing a phone call or anything we choose – to bring us back to our true self, our divine nature. It is a little ironic that these temple bells have become very literal for me.

Every night, as I go to bed, I pop in to my children to give them a final kiss at the end of the day. As they are usually sleeping on their sides, I often kiss them gently on their temples. This has become quite literally, and unintentionally, my temple bell. Every time, I notice the softness of their skin, and the preciousness of the brain that lies within, bringing to life all of the joys, opinions, personality and energy that each child gives every day.

For me, the simple act of placing a kiss on their temples opens up a very strong feeling of awe and appreciation of their indescribable preciousness. This moment is a sacred moment, an unspoken prayer of insight and thanks for what is always there when we slow down enough to see.

Walking as Prayer

I used to run weekend seminars in a venue on Oxford Street in London. As you may know, Oxford Street is one of the busiest streets in London, jammed with traffic and people, shopping, eating or trying to be anywhere but Oxford Street. Very often the traffic moves more slowly than the people on the pavement.

At one point in the seminar I would get participants to do a walking mindful meditation outside, on the street. Mindful walking is an exercise used in many retreats as a way to teach us to slow down, to notice the movements and micro-movements which the body does to balance us and allow us to walk. It teaches us to pay attention to the moment, and to notice our tendency to ignore the journey in our eagerness to get to where we are going. As such it is normally a particularly slow walk, often done within the confines of the room.

However, as fresh air is always welcome and, admittedly, knowing it would also be a little bit of fun, we used to carry out the walking meditation outdoors. Participants would take ten minutes to walk wherever they wished on Oxford Street, slowly and fully consciously, going nowhere in particular, noticing the particulars of everything.

As you can imagine, slow walking was not an easy thing to do considering the environment. And yet so much was learned on every occasion. Participants received many strange looks, and were also stopped by some passers-by and asked if they were okay. Some were approached by police officers concerned for their wellbeing – much to the delight of the group. Not wearing bags or any of the things that normally signal we are on our way somewhere, that we are busy and know what we are about, meant that passers-by had no information to tell them that all was well. Walking in wonder at everything around simply seemed odd to observers.

'Shêmêi pílăo' is a Chinese word meaning aesthetic fatigue. It is another example of how the limitations of our lexicon limit our experience of the world. We have all experienced aesthetic fatigue, whether under-appreciation of the scenery we might pass on our way to work, or walking past some of the greatest works of art in a museum because we have seen enough.

As part of the preparation for the walking meditation, I asked the group to notice that we have habits not only in our thinking, but also in our seeing – we tend to have a habitual line of vision, rarely looking fully downwards, nor more than a few feet above what is straight in front of us. And so I asked the group to raise their gaze upwards to the tops of buildings and the sky, and downwards to the ground. On their return they reported how they noticed that their attention was hijacked by sudden noises or changing traffic signs. Most had observations on things they might never have noticed, lines and markings on the pavement, the workmanship that went into laying the pavements, the brickwork and flowerpots of buildings, and weather patterns in the sky above. But most of all they talked about the fun that comes when we step out of our habitual ways.

Developing a Seven-Day Soul requires us to rouse ourselves out of our aesthetic fatigue, to see again the beauty of everything around us. What might you notice while walking if you were to really pay attention? What behaviours might we forgive in others if we were to slow down enough to wonder how their day is going, how life is for them? We can use the pedestrian lights as a mini-meditation, a practise in patience, choosing to use the wait as a moment to appreciate something or connect with someone, to admire their dog or gently smile, rather than just dashing across the road. The advertisements and instructions at the ATM can be irritating when they are so familiar to us. But again, we can use them as reminders to come back to how we want to live our lives, to very intentionally make the very next thing we do, think or say an act of love.

How To Mindfully Walk

The next time you are walking somewhere:

Take your earphones out. See if you can make eye contact, or give that slight smile of recognition to strangers as you pass. Push yourself to connect with others in an appropriate way – turning to say 'good morning' or whatever feels appropriate as you overtake someone walking, or holding a door open for someone a little longer than might be expected of you. There is not much point in our loveliest intentions for the wellbeing of the planet if we cannot do these simple acts of reconnecting with the people around us.

Be aware that plants, like us, have an inner life, a whole intelligence little understood by us, lived in a time frame different to ours. The fly-eating plant known as a Venus flytrap, the delight of many schoolchildren, can apparently count. Somehow that plant family has come to understand that if it were to close each and every time a fly landed in its jaws, then flies would soon learn that it was not safe to do so. And so the Venus flytrap closes its miniature 'teeth' around only every alternate unfortunate fly, allowing the others to escape. Another fascinating time-lapse video online shows how two climbing plants planted on either side of a stake both grow towards the stake, hoping for its support. When one of the plants reaches the stake and begins to wrap itself around it, the other plant begins to grow away from the stake, in search of support elsewhere.

How is it that the animals that we might see as we walk can each have such individual markings? How is it that the genes of each animal seemingly know to grow perhaps black hair in one body area, and brown or white just an inch away? It is so easy to make throwaway comments about it all being down to genetics, but just how do genes know what to do? What is their life force? Can you connect on your walk with the sense of awe at the incredible complexity and precision of all living things, and parts of things?

If you go into a shop or attend an appointment or meeting, you might notice that the sun has moved in the sky when you return outside. It is so normal to us that it hardly seems worth speaking about. See if you can take just a moment to remember that while you were indoors, our planet continued its path around the sun and rotated on its axis as it went. That seemingly small movement of the sun in the sky is in fact the movement of our planet in space, part of the inherent intelligence that keeps our solar system operating in some cosmic pattern created by nature, not humankind.

Mindfulness in Traffic

When stuck in traffic it can be extremely difficult to think about anything other than getting out of it. But when something is truly out of our control, then choosing a different lens can help to calm the nerves. If we are in a hurry to get somewhere it is so easy to forget that maybe others are too – they are not simply wandering the roads to annoy us.

See if you can imagine a different scenario for the people in each of the cars around you. Try to imagine what their life story might be, why they are on this road and where they are going. What might be on their mind at this time? What worries and sadnesses might they be carrying? This will require some discipline. But if you have children in the car with you, you can use this as a fun family prayer – a great way to show them that prayers are not just what we might say at bedtime but can also be what we do in our day. Concocting enough possible life stories for each of the cars around you is a fun way to teach empathy to your children – and also pass the time!

This exercise or prayer can also be used during a commute on a train, tram or bus. When a carriage is packed and there is nowhere to sit down, use the moment as a temple bell calling you to compassion. When irritation feels justified, let compassion be your prayer.

Mindfulness while Airborne

To some extent, flying is naturally transcendent. It provides us with the bird's-eye view of life that allows us to see things in relation to the wider context. On the ground it is all too easy to become short-sighted, to see only the people that surround us, or the next thing to be done. What is so important to us in everyday life can seem insignificant when airborne.

Take advantage of the opportunity that flying provides to sit for a time and review your life. For most of us flying is not a regular activity so it naturally takes us out of routine and opens up a space for contemplation. Is your life heading where you really want it to go? What effects are you having on the people you come into contact with? What will be the space that you leave as your legacy? How might what you buy and what you do affect people in other countries? How much plastic do you use? Are there things you could do differently to reduce the amount of plastic you discard? How are you treating other species? Often the answers are not far below the surface of our minds and come to us easily when we stop long enough to listen. But it is well worthwhile writing down what comes to you in a diary or some other place that you will see regularly. Don't leave these ideas that represent your values in a notebook you will never return to. Your life is far too important for that.

Often the major issues of the world, like poverty and war, seem just too big for us to even consider tackling. A great way to pass the time on board is to list some of the issues that most of us would normally leave to politicians or the most powerful or wealthy in the world. Take one issue that interests you. Let's say you choose poverty. Poverty affects millions of people worldwide, which is why we tend to withdraw in defeat. But instead, this time, choose one country or place and see what you can find out about the causes of poverty there.

As you fly, choose to take one group of people under your wing, to make them your responsibility. You might work to link your home town with a specific town in a poor area at home or abroad, or research the most cost-efficient charities working in the area to support. You might decide that you will write to politicians to encourage them to act or choose to refuse to buy particular goods if their production harms other people. You might research volunteering opportunities with a particular agency or how best to introduce your family to vegetarian meals for the sake of animals and the planet. Perhaps you could take the time to get more specific about exactly how much time and exactly how much money you can give to charitable work.

Often the magnitude of the world's problems can overwhelm us to the point of inaction. We can be so bombarded with requests for money that many of us never feel any specific tie to, let alone responsibility for, any one group of people in need. Whatever you choose as your next step, see if it is possible for you to narrow down your focus to one or a small number of issues which you could stick with for the medium to long term – to make them your responsibility, at least partially. Stick a marker in the map to say that this is the group that you will help – that your existence *will* have an impact on.

Mindfulness in Conversation: Moving Beyond Instinctive Habit

There is a guilty satisfaction that can come with speaking ill of other people. It can feel like a weight has been lifted off our shoulders when we share our irritations with someone else. The sense of shared connection it can create between the speaker and the listener can act as a show of openness to the other, indicating that we trust them enough to confide in them.

This reaches deep into the history of our brain, tickling its most primitive areas that hold our tribal tendencies, our need to link with others, to share our information and to receive the acceptance of others. It taps into our need to belong, to be part of the pack, where we can be safe. Sharing our less than wholesome opinions with someone is a way of inviting them to connect with our tribe. On a more conscious level, it can feel flattering to be confided in, to be included in someone's inner circle.

But we are more than mere animals. We are more than a collection of drives and instincts. We are in a process of evolution towards the outing of our divine nature, our sacred selves. Our task is to be fully responsible for our part in this next spiritual evolution and as such, we must constantly check how we our doing.

It is certainly true that a problem shared can be a problem halved. But we need to be careful with whom we share our feelings about another person. Checking in with our motivations will tell us if we are truly looking for emotional support, or if we are unconsciously buying social connection or status within a conversation. We all need our wall to talk to, the person who can hear our frustrations, but who can be trusted to never repeat what we have said, nor give too much weight to our emotive opinions; someone to hear us, without giving legs to our outpourings. But when we know in our heart of hearts that we are simply giving out because it feels good, or in order to denigrate another human being, then we need to do our best to tell it to the wind – and the wind alone.

'Great minds discuss ideas;
Average minds discuss events;
Small minds discuss people.'
— Eleanor Roosevelt

Mindfulness at the Desk

At the desk, as in all the doings of the day, there are always opportunities to practise the chosen Seven-Day Soul pillar.

We can use the time it takes for our PC to warm up as an opportunity to simply take a breath, perhaps reminding ourselves of the preciousness of life, or to look at the work piled up on our desk and think of those who scramble through scrapheaps collecting bones and bottles to sell at the market. If world economics were to reverse, would any of us have earned the right to ask them for their help based on what we have done for them?

We often think of stillness as requiring extended periods of sitting in meditation, but stillness can also mean being fully engaged in a conversation, fully listening, our attention unmoving from the other person. It can mean the ability to stay present enough to leave a pause before responding, not in some pretence of a monk-like self-awareness but in honest listening, absorbing the perspective of the other.

We can be generous with our time, asking one more

question than we normally would about someone else's opinion, or seeing if it is possible for us to forgive a mistake by someone, calling to mind the things that we would also like to be forgiven for. We can give a smile or show warmth in the way we phrase an email, and avoid the temptation to make a power play when it feels like the easiest response.

We can choose to share kind words with and show openness in our manner. We can be generous with our laughter, even when it is not humour's pillar day. Most of us don't appreciate humour as nature's clever antidote to stress and tension – a lovely release valve for body and mind, a therapy of social connection. In a single second we can appreciate how it lightens our emotional load.

The paper in the books on our desks can connect us to a forest somewhere where once that tree was planted, harvested and made into paper in a mill in which people are possibly still working today. In those pages is sunlight, the carbon dioxide breathed by the tree and the nutrients from the soil that nourished the tree. The tea or coffee that you drink came from somewhere probably very far away from where you are now; the milk, from a cow, or perhaps a plant somewhere unknown. The desk where you sit has been carved or moulded during the working day of others. What might their worries be for themselves and their loved ones?

Transcending time and the limitations of our immediately visible environment connects us with the Something Much Greater than we understand, and our lives become far more than an endless calendar of empty days. If these activities seem too otherworldly or only for those with time on their hands, remember that they can be done in a moment or two by literally 'sparing a thought for' as we go through the day. There is no need to even stop as you do so – you will have automatically changed your lens on the world to a wider, self-transcendent context. But don't be fooled by the simplicity of these exercises – progress is built on repetitions, not respite.

Each pillar of the Seven-Day Soul is an exercise in 'agape'. Agape is a Greek word for a type of love which the ancient Greeks differentiated from romantic love (eros) and love of family and brotherhood/ sisterhood (philia). Agape describes the highest form of love we can know, the act of loving something that is unlikeable, a love that is unmerited or unearned by the recipient, but which is given anyway.

As such, agape is used to describe the love of God in the Christian tradition, but it really represents the aim in life for every one of us – or at least it should. It is the pinnacle of how to live, and the lesson of our whole existence. Like 'love', it is a small word and a big task. It sounds like an attractive idea but in practise it's incredibly difficult. This is why we very consciously practise a way of exercising agape in its various forms in the Seven-Day Soul's pillars: we try to forgive when it is unasked for, to be generous when it is unearned. Gratitude reminds us that we are also receiving agape, that we have no real claim to the luxuries we have in our lives, but receive them unmerited. Patience gives us the grit to stick with our efforts to evolve, awe hydrates us, and humour carries us.

Over the coming chapters, we begin to widen the circle of effect in our practise of agape, from family life outward to the rest of the world. The challenges will naturally become more difficult – but the impact we effect on our collective consciousness will be even greater.

8

Expanding Our Gears of Consciousness

'The key to growth is the introduction of higher dimensions of consciousness into our awareness.'
— **Lao Tzu**

Consciousness, the space in which thinking takes place, is the new frontier of science. It reaches into theology, psychology, philosophy, neuroscience, quantum physics and other fields of research, so it is not surprising that we have great hopes for it to be the place in which we finally find the explanation for our existence or perhaps God.

Whether this turns out to be true or misguided, what is certainly true is that we need to understand our consciousness better, to expand our repertoire of lenses on the world, so that we might take our noses from the grindstone and see the ultimate context in which we live our lives.

All major religions have teachings about levels of consciousness or spirit in all things animal, vegetable and mineral. These levels of consciousness are really describing degrees of separation from ultimate reality, degrees of filtration from ultimate truth. There is really only one truth, but many degrees of blindness to it.

Imagine trying to eavesdrop on a conversation taking place in a room in your house. If you are on a different level in the house, you might hear noise that you can recognise as voices but little else. If you move closer to the conversation, perhaps to a nearby room on the same floor, the voices are still being filtered through the walls, but maybe you can hear a little more than before – you might grasp the loudest parts of the conversation, or laughter. If you come to stand just outside the door, you will probably be able to recognise who is speaking and hear most of what is being said. But when you enter the room, everything becomes fully clear to you. It is the same with our levels of understanding of our universe.

The task for us all in developing our Seven-Day Soul is the task set for humanity: to work to decrease this separation from the eternal truth, this ultimate explanation of everything. When we do, we will have achieved enlightenment, Nirvana; we will have put on the mind of Christ. This is the ultimate purpose of our lives, and the aim of human evolution according to the teachings of some of the world's greatest wisdom mentors.

What We Do, We Become

The Western mind seems to have arrived at a point in which we value only a small bandwidth of consciousness, a chosen few gears of consciousness that we utilise regularly in our busy lives. But what we do, we become.

Our brain cells communicate with each other by synaptic transmission, whereby one brain cell transmits a chemical called a neurotransmitter, which carries chemical information to the neighbouring neuron, which in turn sets off its own chemical communication with the next neuron. Electrical impulses are also passed from one neuron to another, at a much faster rate than the chemical communication. This electrical communication is called 'neural firing'.

In 1949, neuropsychologist Donald Hebb coined the phrase 'neurons that fire together, wire together'. It's a catchy phrase that summarises a hugely important finding: when a set of neurons repeatedly send and receive messages between each other, these neurons become more strongly connected, so that the brain becomes more likely to fire off this neural communication again – a sort of neural superhighway.

Repeated connection between a set of neurons leads to a well-worn path of communication between this set of neurons and the development of all our automatic behaviours. This is why some of us spend hours hitting golf balls on the driving range, why a child practises their musical scales repeatedly on the piano, and why it can be so hard to keep our new year's resolutions – we don't give them enough repetition to become the 'new me'. But when we do, we build connections between the neurons that correspond in the brain to our desired behaviour, and it becomes more likely that the brain will set in motion that perfect golf swing. Let's not forget that we have habits not just in what we do, but also in what we think and what we feel. In the words of Mahatma Gandhi:

> *Your beliefs become your thoughts,*
> *Your thoughts become your words,*
> *Your words become your actions,*
> *Your actions become your habits,*
> *Your habits become your values,*
> *Your values become your destiny.*

It is not just the individual, but also society as a whole, that has a habitual way of viewing the world. The prioritising of understanding the world through logic and analysis began back in the days of the Enlightenment, and has been re-wiring the human brain ever since. In his wonderful book *The Master and His Emissary*, psychiatrist Dr Iain McGilchrist explains how our society has become wired to interpret the world through the primarily analytical style of the left hemisphere.

If we were to hold a human brain we would see that

it is comprised of two halves (hemispheres), connected in the middle by a body of 300–800 million neural fibres, which allows each hemisphere to partly help and partly hinder the other – something akin to the love you today/hate you tomorrow relationship of squabbling siblings. While it is true that almost all activities require input from both hemispheres, research collected by McGilchrist shows that the two work in utterly different ways, and each has a completely different take on the world around us. The difference is in 'how' not 'what', they do; how they spend our limited budget of attention. Most of this research comes from studies of patients who have suffered a stroke or damage to one side of the brain. The left and right hemispheres have a different take on reality, with the left tending to narrow things down to certainty, while the right opens up to possibility. This tendency of the left to narrow things down to certainty has its uses, in that it helps us to function in the world, to be able to grasp it.

In looking for certainty, the left hemisphere renders everything explicit, knowable; while the right tends to comprehend the implicit nature of the world, the more nebulous, un-graspable information between the 'facts': irony, humour and the subtleties of body language. Most of us will have had the experience of knowing that what was being said explicitly was not what was meant implicitly. The tone of voice of a barbed tongue can make the implicit message very different to what is said explicitly.

The left hemisphere collapses the world of probability so that it can appear certain to us; the right is better able to deal with possibilities and unknowing. The left sees the parts, while the right sees the whole; the left sees things as fixed, while the right prefers flow.

We begin to see the pattern emerging of the left hemisphere seeing the world as if everything in it is made of separate atoms, each distinct from the other, things seen in abstraction rather than part of a bigger whole. This mechanistic world view results in our seeing the world as something separate to us, like a machine that we can manipulate at will. We are all familiar with this view of the world – we do not normally feel at one with the computer, book or table.

The left hemisphere is also more optimistic and appears almost more 'self-assured', in that neural communication between the two lobes travels mostly from left to right, so that the right hemisphere receives the balancing effects of input from the left hemisphere to a greater extent than the left receives input from the right.

Driven mostly by a nature more typical of our left hemisphere, we too prefer people who think like us, and struggle to welcome conflicting opinions or personalities. Anyone who has ever sat around a boardroom or dinner table knows that it is quite a challenge to give anything more than lip service to welcoming new ideas that don't fit with our own. It is not an easy thing to honestly welcome ideas that go against what we believe to be true.

In neural imaging studies, scientists can view in real time the world as viewed through the two hemispheres, the right mostly involved with things that are new to us, and 'seeing anew' each event, instant, word, or musical note while they are still novel and fresh, allowing us to remain present to each moment in its newness and uniqueness. Incoming information moves from the right hemisphere to the left as it becomes more familiar to us, where it gets collated into more generalised concepts, a sort of mental filing system, so that we can connect the information to what we already know.

Studies have shown the left hemisphere to have a tendency to be speedier, but also more prone to making mistakes. Activity in the right hemisphere is slower and broader. It is always interested in the uniqueness; the left, in the generality of things.

So how does this understanding of the left and right brain hemispheres affect how we might mainstream spiritual living back into society? Since the days of the Enlightenment, society began to veer towards a preference for the left's atomised perspective on the world – a world made up of lots of parts rather than an interacting system.

From the seventeenth and eighteenth centuries

onwards, the Greek word 'psyche' changed from meaning both the spirit essence or whole of a person to just the operations of the mind. At the same time, we began to look upon the world as a giant mechanism to be manipulated by us, rather than the gods, and humankind separated itself from nature. It was during this period of history that the right hemisphere's ability to see things in their larger context, as part of the whole, was side-lined. We lost the ability to appreciate the abstract and instead generalised everything so that it lost nuance but became measurable.

These mechanistic ways of seeing the world work well for us in much of our day-to-day living. But when we look up and begin to wonder why we are here, what is the point of all our efforts and how might we know God better, it is then that we need the big picture lens provided more fully by the right lobe.

If we were to imagine drawing our life as a straight line on a page, we could choose to evaluate it according to the events of our life, as if our life is nothing more than a to-do list. But we know that life isn't like that. All of our to-do's are animated by a purpose we aim for, or by something in the broader context of the page our life is drawn on. We might go to work not just to put food on the table, but because we derive a sense of personal satisfaction from our work, or are driven to give our children a better chance at life than we had growing up. We might keep a tatty old armchair because it reminds us of someone who used to sit in it. We might increase our exercise not because we personally want to get fit but because we want to set a good example for our children. We go to a film we don't like because someone we care about needs company.

We already do these things of no apparent value because of their wider context. If we are serious about our role in creating change in the world, then we need to see everything we do in the wider context of love. Seeing the rest of the page as being full of God, love, or a higher purpose we are heading towards will give meaning to everything we do, no matter how seemingly small, because it relates it in some way to that bigger picture.

This is why it is so important to understand our gears of consciousness, to learn to recognise and move in and out of different lenses on the world. If we are working on something or speaking with someone, our focus will narrow down to what we are doing or saying, and this is entirely appropriate. But we also need to be conscious enough to be able to choose a different lens through which to view the world by way of activating the other hemisphere of the brain. In moving from an activation of the left hemisphere to the right, we see the world in its relatedness, a system of interactiveness. We see the 'between-ness' of things and the importance of love.

This between-ness is easiest to understand in music, where no single note creates the beauty of the whole. Similarly, if we stand an adult and child side by side, we might notice differences in height, clothing, voice and even levels of wisdom. But if this adult and child are father and child, then it is not these differences that are important, but that which is between them; that the adult might live and die for that child, connected by a love that resides not completely in either the adult or the child, but in the between-ness of them both. When we look in this space, with this cognitive lens, we see the related-ness, the real meaning in the image.

It is with this broader lens that we find the gestalt of things, the ability to see everything in relation to something bigger, the figure and the ground. And it is with this gestalt lens that we will find the meaning of our lives; the ability to see everything we do in relation to a larger meaning, that transcends but incorporates the self into its wider context.

The value of this between-ness is beautifully explained by Mal, a workshop participant who wanted to go further in bringing spirituality into his life. Mal was married with two children and worked as a self-employed landscape gardener. He operated from a small office at home, travelling to clients in a pick-up truck, sometimes with another man who helped out when needed. As such, Mal felt that he didn't get much opportunity to connect with people.

When we first did the exercise about listing the things I do in my day along a line, I was pretty sure even you [the author] would agree that I don't see a huge number of people in my day. Of course I send emails and make calls, but because I work alone most of the time it is hard to see how much impact I can have on the world.

But then we did that 'between-ness' exercise, where we filled in all the spaces between the things I do during the day. I remember I hadn't even listed my kids and my wife in the morning – I was focused on being kind to other people! I didn't think of the postman who I see almost every morning (now I make an effort to open the door to shout 'thanks' to him) and the neighbours that I wave to when putting out the bins. I didn't count other people in traffic, and I definitely had never said a prayer for pedestrians crossing the road in front of me! I never thought about how people all around me all had suffering. I had thought about the people I bought my plants from, but hadn't thought about the growers I never met. Their work is so important to mine and it was really good to remember this.

I began to give feedback to the people I did have contact with and asked that my thanks be passed on to the other growers. I would always have said 'thank you', but that's just what everyone says. It had become kind of meaningless, so I really tried to say much more than that.

I'm pretty good about being careful to respect animal habitats as much as I can, but I think I also got better at this too – as much as I can – although I do have to kill some critters!

Once we had done this exercise, I began to see more and more ways in which I was connected into things. Even thinking about the people who made my phone that I use all the time, my laptop, my food, etc. On the phone I really tried to say something kind or to ask a question about how people were – without sounding weird!

It even helped to see what I cook for the kids as being like plant feed – nourishing their roots. It made it a little easier to put some effort into what I give them to eat when I'm cooking. As you said, parenting can seem like a slow-burn process, so it was really good to take that 'big lens' view of their childhood, and realise that their ten and seven years of life so far are made up of all the dinners, lunches and so on that seemed boring and dull at the time. It all matters in the 'big lens picture'. I may not be enlightened – but at least I'm wearing bi-focals now!

The collective consciousness we operate in is a self-perpetuating one that fails to see its own limitations. Without the counterbalancing of the right hemispheric lens on the world, which would allow us to more easily find meaning and the larger context of our lives, the mechanical style of the left hemisphere becomes the default mode of our thinking.

This happens without our knowledge. It takes the self-awareness of the right-brain to see how we are thinking, but it is exactly this lens that is being omitted, and so the narrow, atomistic, mechanistic way of interacting with the world rolls on.

'The intuitive mind is a sacred gift, and the rational mind a faithful servant. We have created a society that honours the servant and has forgotten the gift.'
– attributed to Albert Einstein

What Are We Not Seeing?

The human body is an unreliable interpretive centre, which would better be described as a filter, rather than a lens, on the world. Apart from the limitations of our senses, even what is seen and heard is filtered through our previous biases, expectations, habits and preferences. In this way, our view of reality is double filtered. While science tells us that there are perhaps an infinite number of dimensions, our bandwidth is attuned to just three, and we know nothing of the rest.

Spiritual growth demands that we become fully aware that there is more to the world than what we see.

In an interesting but cruel study, researchers studying how visual capabilities develop in the brain divided kittens into two groups – a horizontal world group and a vertical world group.

The vertical group was raised in a world of vertical lines only – the wallpaper inside their cages was black and white stripe, their handlers wore either solid colours or vertical stripes. In the other group, the kittens saw nothing but horizontal lines inside their cages and on their handlers.

The animals were kept in these conditions for the first serval weeks of their lives. When they were eventually taken out, the results were striking. The kittens raised in the horizontal lines environment were able to see horizontal lines in the world, like the seat of a chair. They could jump up and curl up on the seat, but were blind to its vertical legs. The other group were able to avoid the legs or curl themselves neatly around them, but never saw the seat above them.

From a neurological point of view, we see the world in lines, made up of stick figures recognisable by the arrangement of horizontal and vertical lines. The brains of the kittens had missed the critical window for the neural development of either vertical or horizontal lines, and the animals were never able to see what was right in front of them.

In brain terms, what we don't use gets dumped. It's a process called neural pruning where, much like the common or garden variety of pruning, the brain prunes off neurons that are not used. In the case of the kittens, the neurons involved in the recognition of either vertical or horizontal lines were never activated and were pruned.

When we are raised in a culture that breeds us to value above all else materialism, fact-ism and individualism, we are made blind to other aspects of the world. Even if they could talk, the kittens would not ask to be shown the lines they can't see because, as the rest of their vision works perfectly, they wouldn't know that there exist things which they cannot see.

The rise of depression, suicide, and experiencing feelings of meaninglessness is our version of banging into the legs of chairs. We need to heed it as a big wake-up call. Whole nations and continents are just larger replicas of this same process of personal and cultural blindness. We must as a society revisit the teachings of all the wisdom traditions that have stood the test of time; teachings on compassion, love and self-transcendence; on accessing states of consciousness that we are not familiar with. Lessons on the interconnectedness of us all. We are not the solid, closed system entities we view ourselves to be, with clear boundaries between what is me and the external world. We are porous, permeable, open-looped systems, born to self-transcend and to love. It is here that we find the meaning of our life.

To Be and Not To Be

Today we know that in the very tiny world of quantum mechanics, tiny particles called quanta, far smaller in size than atoms, behave in ways that do not obey the laws of physics we are accustomed to.

Two quanta, at any distance apart, seem to communicate with each other at speeds far faster than the speed of light, an event which Albert Einstein dubbed 'spooky action at a distance'. This is completely contrary to the laws of classical physics which govern most of our everyday living. As we have seen, light has been shown to not only travel in waves but also in particles and, even more spookily, seems to behave differently when observed.

It seems that when scientists work at sizes millions of times smaller than the atom, the world is made up mostly of space, and that the quanta or building blocks by which the world is made behave in ways that contradict how we experience the world as we see it. In fact, according to the laws of quantum physics, the act of observation changes reality. Before anything is observed, an event has neither happened nor not happened, but is in two states at the same time, a mathematical concept called a superposition. Only when the wave is observed (or measured) does it 'collapse' into a state of either happening or not happening. In this way, the consciousness of observation causes the reality we see.

We could say that our senses also collapse sound waves into sound, and the reflection of light into sight. We are never simply receiving pure reality without interpretation.

Some physicists have proposed an alternative theory in which the universe to split into two different universes, one in which the event happened, and the other in which it did not. This became known as the 'multiverse theory'. In this theory, every possible event in the world does and doesn't happen, with each alternative splitting the world into another parallel universe.

No matter which theory any of us might choose, it is generally accepted that the world we live in is in fact a quantum world where these strange events do indeed occur. But at some point between the tiny world of quantum physics and the world as we normally see it, the laws of quantum physics that allow these strange events to occur give way to the laws of classical physics that we are familiar with.

According to many physicists, we cannot know the world directly, but only secondary to our sense perceptions – or the limitations of our senses. Limitations of our consciousness, and our mental interpretations of time, space and duality, separate us from a dimension that can answer our existential questions.

'I regard consciousness as fundamental. I regard matter as a derivative of consciousness.'
– Max Planck, Nobel Prize-winning physicist (1918)

On Time: When Now Is So Last Year

In our day-to-day lives we experience time as flowing or moving in a way we sometimes describe as the 'arrow of time'. But in the quantum world, time does not move, but only feels like it does because of the mechanisms in our mind. In the 'real' external world, there is no such movement.

We also think of physical space as having three dimensions, but in fact there is actually no evidence of this. Einstein's theory of general relativity also showed that we should really view all of space, including the vastness of outer space, as space-time, and that like a trampoline mat that bends when we stand on it, space-time can also be bent by large objects such as planets.

So to summarise, the arrow of time isn't straight, isn't moving, and isn't an arrow. Space isn't space, but space-time. Time as we know it is due to the deceptions of our perception, which are incomplete and sometimes inaccurate representations that our minds use to make sense of the world around us.

These mistakes in the way we understand the world have kept philosophers in business for centuries. But the relatively recent scientific findings in the field of quantum mechanics are shedding new light on the subject, and helping to support the idea that we have a very limited ability to perceive everything in the world and that our life's purpose is to shed these limitations. Teachings on Nirvana, salvation and the celestial kingdom are all related to this idea of arriving at full understanding. And our understanding of time seems to be key:

'If a soul is to see God it must look at nothing in time;
For while the soul is occupied with time or place or any image of the kind, it cannot recognise God.'
– Meister Eckhart, Christian mystic

In Buddhist thought, our task is also to rid ourselves of all of these mistakes of the mind, that give us a sense of me and non-me, you versus me. For Buddhists, the very idea of thinking 'about' anything automatically separates us from being one with it, by creating words to describe it.

Time, for the Buddhist, is also a creation of the mind. Consciousness and time cannot be separated, firstly because in Buddhist teaching everything is ultimately one, but also because consciousness happens in time. Our sense of past, present and future all occur in the now, but appear separated because of the mechanics of our mind.

In an interview in 1934, award-winning physicist, astronomer and mathematician Sir James Jeans was asked, 'Do you believe that life on this planet is the result of some sort of accident, or do you believe that it is a part of some great scheme?'

Jeans replied:

I incline to the idealistic theory that consciousness is fundamental, and that the material universe is derivative from consciousness, not consciousness from the material universe . . . In general the universe seems to me to be nearer to a great thought than to a great machine. It may well be, it seems to me, that each individual consciousness ought to be compared to a brain-cell in a universal mind.

What remains is in any case very different from the full-blooded matter and the forbidding materialism of the Victorian scientist. His objective and material universe is proved to consist of little more than constructs of our own minds. To this extent, then, modern physics has moved in the direction of philosophic idealism. Mind and matter, if not proved to be of similar nature, are at least found to be ingredients of one single system. There is no longer room for the kind of dualism which has haunted philosophy since the days of Descartes.

'Our normal waking consciousness, rational consciousness as we call it, is but one special type of consciousness, whilst all about it, parted by the filmiest of screens, there lie potential forms of consciousness entirely different.'
–William James, father of modern psychology

In the Hindu tradition, this 'filmiest of screens' is known as 'the veil of Maya', that film between us and the one truth which causes our experience of duality and separation. In Hinduism, the universe is thought to emerge out of consciousness, and our aim as human beings is to become one with this consciousness.

In the eighteenth century, the German philosopher Arthur Schopenhauer said that if we as human beings learned to step out of our notions of space and time, then we would be able to break through this veil, and rid ourselves of the illusion of our individuality.

Christian teachings on heaven could also be interpreted to mean humanity's growth out of our current limitations in perception, by way of love. If we 'love thy neighbour as thyself', would this be the second coming of Christ? Heaven's eternity, then, might be time-lessness rather than forever-ness – an existence no longer limited by our usual understanding of time or space.

It isn't easy to change our habitual way of understanding the dimensions of time and space – as we have seen, this way of thinking is now physically hard-wired into our minds. Learning to undo this worldview will require us all to re-evaluate the lesser-known modes of mind – along with perhaps generations of practise. But even a short review of the gears of consciousness which we already know can help us to become more aware that we already switch between lenses on the world.

Ask yourself the following questions:

* Have you ever been so engrossed in a film that you jumped when something scary happened, even though your eyes could also see the surround of the television and perhaps some of your sitting room?

* Have you ever been enjoying yourself so much that you were shocked at how much time had passed?

* Have you ever felt like every minute seems like an hour – such as waiting to receive a phone call from someone special?

* Have you ever done something that you felt embarrassed about immediately afterwards because you just 'forgot where you were'?

* Have you ever been asleep?

* Have you ever been unconscious? Or under general anaesthesia?

✳ Have you ever been so engrossed in a task that challenged you just enough that you lost track of time, your location, and the ability to be aware of your own thoughts? This is a state called 'flow' – as soon as you become aware that you have been in flow, you have come out of that state.

✳ Have you ever consciously chosen to concentrate hard on something – to narrow down your focus of attention? This type of concentration is different to the state of flow, as in this instance you are consciously choosing to keep your attention on the job and you have not lost your self-awareness.

✳ Have you ever done something on autopilot?

✳ Have you ever been blindfolded and spun around, for example as a child, so that you lose your sense of direction?

✳ Have you ever had a daydream?

✳ Have you ever been so relaxed that you just chilled and allowed your mind to drift off to imaginary other places?

✳ Has a smell ever triggered a memory for you, and suddenly it feels like you are back in that time?

* Have you ever sleepwalked?

* Have you ever practised mindful awareness of the present moment?

* Have you ever entered a state of hypnosis, where images and suggestions of different times and places felt completely real to you?

There are many, many examples of the different states of consciousness that we move in and out of regularly in our lives. Some of these we choose, and others are triggered by the environment or by someone else. See if you can become more aware of the states of consciousness you most often pass through, keeping in mind that as soon as you become aware of a particular state, you are probably no longer in that state.

Learning to live spiritually means living in relationship to something greater than ourselves, something perhaps intangible but not completely unknowable. As the wisdom and religious traditions have been telling us for centuries, learning to move adeptly between these states of consciousness, opting in and out of left and right hemispheric ways of thinking, will expand our repertoire of ways of seeing. In so doing, these traditions tell us that we will learn to see the larger context of our existence, the ultimate truth behind everything that is, and the ground of love.

9

Spirituality in Parenting and Family Life

'You are the bows from which your children as
living arrows are sent forth . . .
Let your bending in the Archer's hand
be for gladness; For even as He loves the arrow that
flies, so He loves also the bow that is stable.'
— *On Children*, Kahlil Gibran

On the wall in front of my desk, alongside a picture of a flying pig, sits a postcard depicting a marble sculpture of an infant playfully climbing on his mother's back, kissing her face as she looks back at him.

The seeming contradiction of the cold marble carved by Edward Hodges Baily (1788–1867) into such an incredibly tender moment is something that can hold my attention long after I should be head down at the keyboard. The infant holds the mother's face and the mother gently supports her son in his precarious position. It's a capture of a precious moment that I have had the privilege to experience, and it's perhaps because of this that the sculpture transports me. I often wonder if the child is lying on the mother's hair and slightly hurting her, but she doesn't want to ruin the moment by moving her head. Does the child's kiss swallow her into the present in a way that months of meditation could not do? Are all the tasks and chores that she must do demoted in the preciousness of the kiss? Is it she who is being taught the power of being loved unconditionally, or her child?

Parenthood has moments like these, that can grab us by the collar into a sense of the universal, but more often it can seem a far more mundane and gloss-less task.

Urban wisdom suggests that you should write the book on parenting before you have children, when you still think you know it all. As parents, many of us have to come to terms with the possibility that we are not always the parents we want to be. Alongside the guru-ification of just about every aspect of life has come the notion that we should parent as if we are therapists, and that we should speak to our children as if they are our clients. Quality time, like the rest of our children's lives, must be scheduled into the day. For most of us, when we don't quite manage to do it all, parenting can feel like the greatest lesson in humility we have ever had.

But parenting is a fully sacred path, no lesser than

any formal religious role, and is in fact the perfect practise ground for the evolution of our Seven-Day Soul. Nothing crash-lands us into self-transcendence quite the way parenting does.

From the moment of a child's birth to their leaving the home, and indeed beyond, parenting is unique in its ability to offer us a way to develop ourselves and another (or others) simultaneously.

When we see it in this light, it is not surprising that it is as challenging and difficult as anything with such huge rewards can be. We are being charged with a piece of creation. It is society in miniature, society in its seed form – today's children are tomorrow's parents. But in the immediacy and dullness of yet another school lunch, the endless balancing act between work and family, or taxiing of our children from one point to another, the stewardship of the divine aspect of our children can be a million miles from our thoughts. Only by conscious effort can we anchor and re-anchor our role as parent back into the gestalt view of life, where the grubby, repetitive tasks of the day find their ultimate meaning.

Parenting is a slow-burn, long-term results project with little in the way of immediate feedback on how we are doing. Childbirth can feel like its first and last spiritual moment. Much like faith, parenthood is a risk that requires courage. But if spiritual and religious beliefs are kept for just one day a week then they are worth nothing. It is our everyday life that is, or is not, our spirituality. In parenting, we are given the opportunity to practise trying to live from a more cosmic perspective, to put on the mind of Christ, to work towards enlightenment and to make our lives meaningful. It is also, to paraphrase the famous American psychotherapist Dr Ira Progoff, an opportunity to nurture a seed before we know what it will grow to be.

The Paper-Thin Life

In our wealthy Western culture, most of us are lucky enough to have our most basic needs for food, water and safety covered. A smaller, but still sizeable number have their needs for status and achievement also fulfilled.

If we have grown up without having strived for any of these things, it is easy to place little value on them. When this happens, a person can feel that something is missing from their life. They may simply live with a feeling that life is a dull, repetitive treadmill, or presume that feeling down is just a natural part of life.

Introducing our children to another way of considering their existence, another dimension to their being in the world, gives them a whole new lexicon of ways to understand themselves. It gives them a spiritual vocabulary. When life feels empty or they are experiencing a void in their life, when life feels meaningless or they cannot find their place in the world, the spiritually educated individual has additional ways of understanding these feelings. They know that they have noetic as well as physical and psychological needs and that these feelings might best be addressed from a spiritual perspective.

'Every child has their own shine.'
— From *Meditation with Children*
by Dr Noel Keating

Most of us have been raised with the idea that prayer is something which starts and ends with blessing ourselves, with the recitation of a prayer — often made up of someone else's words — in between. But when we think of the two planes of our spiritual life, the vertical plane of meditation and stillness, and the horizontal plane of our active living, we get a whole menu of options of ways to pray.

You do not have to set aside special times for prayer if you struggle to do so — or if your children aren't interested. Your very attention is an act of prayer and an act of active awareness, because paying attention to someone fully and completely in the moment takes our heads out of thinking about the past and the future, deep into the vastness of the now. When we pay attention to someone in the moment, we recognise the universal, ultimate, holy dimension of every moment, outside of our normal understanding of past and future. Giving our attention fully to someone is giving recognition to their place in the universe and God's plan. It is diving deeply beneath the surface. The same is true, perhaps even more true, of giving our attention to someone we struggle to like, or even our spouse or partner when we have grown over-familiar and under-appreciative.

'Do as I say, not as I do' is a phrase that most of us can relate to. Our hopes for our children often aim higher than we ourselves have managed. But as anyone who has ever glimpsed their own foible, intonation, or turn of phrase in their child will testify, our children learn from what they see us do. How we treat and interact with our spouse or partner then becomes every bit as important a life lesson as the things we tell our children. It is perhaps the first and most repeated lesson they will ever witness in their lives, so it is important that the two people in a partnership or marriage play their part to the very best of their ability.

I am reminded of one of my workshops at which all the attendees were psychotherapists. The group had been talking about the fact that really listening is an act of giving. The next day, one woman stood up to say that she had gone home the previous evening and had noticed that when she walked into the kitchen, her husband was emptying the dishwasher and putting things into the cupboards. As she started to tell him about her day, her husband stopped what he was doing and turned to listen to her. She noticed his listening, and it dawned on her that, had she been emptying the dishwasher, she would have kept on going, probably listening to him 'through the back of her head'. What was more shocking to her was the fact that as a psychotherapist, she was professionally trained to listen!

Most of us can relate to having some degree of social mask which we wear when not at home, and to letting it slip when we get home. All of our best listening, manners, patience and selflessness is frequently spent by the time we arrive home from work, so it can often be that it is the people we would otherwise die for who get what's left of our energies, the very worst part of ourselves.

Sometimes it can feel like we are clinging on to marriage like a raft, not quite fully on board nor sure about where we're headed, a sort of wait and see approach. But when we marry, we are supposed to be tying the knot, not trying the knot. We need to see marriage and committed relationships as living entities which require looking after, tending to and re-directing when necessary. If you are in a committed relationship you probably did this very well at the beginning – you were complimentary to your partner, generous, communicative and loving. But after years together, it can be easy to fall into treating our partners like a ticked box: sorted, done, what's next on the to-do list?

Re-remembering the divine nature of our partner can be a useful way to reignite or nurture a relationship. We need to remember they have a direct relationship with God or the Ultimate Truth that does not involve us. We are just lucky enough to witness it.

Have you ever considered your partner's spiritual life? Have you ever asked them where they find spiritual fulfilment? It may be very different to yours, and your partner might struggle to find appropriate language to give you an answer, or even to understand the question. But don't let this put you off. Sometimes shared experiences can help us to understand the things that cannot be conceptualised into words. Sharing opportunities for that deep feeling of peace, stillness, gratitude, authenticity or connection can communicate the existence of our spiritual self, much more than words. Developing a family awareness of things to be grateful for is a good place to begin increasing your family's spiritual life.

> **'No human being can ever 'own' another whether in friendship, love, marriage or parenthood. Many human relationships have been ruined and happiness for too long changed to misery by a failure to understand this.'**
>
> **– Eleanor Roosevelt**

Saying grace before a meal is a way of showing gratitude for the food we are about to enjoy. Traditionally, grace involved blessing oneself and then saying a short, usually pre-learned prayer, often the same one each evening, and a sign of the cross to sort of close it off. The very effort of saying the prayer was the prayer.

But you could just as easily ask everyone around the table what they are grateful for that day. It is up to you whether or not you choose to say 'grateful to God' or simply just 'grateful'. It can be difficult to sincerely feel grateful for something like a hot meal that we often take for granted unless it is something you do not get to enjoy often. Getting everyone around the table to say something that they are grateful for from their day can be a better way of ensuring it is a sincere prayer of gratitude. It means that you are enhancing your children's spiritual education in a way that teaches them that spirituality is a 'do-ing' rather than just a 'thinking'. It is also less alienating for teenage children who might be struggling with traditionally taught prayers.

There are of course no rules to prayers (and you don't have to use the word 'prayer' if that jars with some people at the table), but it is a good idea to suggest that everyone should try to mention a different thing they are grateful for each day. This means that after a few days of mentioning some of the more obvious things we might be grateful for, like our health, our family, and so on, we get to a stage where each person needs to have their radar on to notice things or events in their day to be grateful for. Simply noticing that they got lots of green traffic lights when they were hurrying somewhere in the car signals the beginning of waking up to what is already here.

But just a word to the wise: no one should ever feel under pressure to participate in this prayer of thanks. I remember one evening my ten-year-old saying that he was grateful that the next day was Friday as I always forgot to ask them what they were grateful for on a Friday!

Through the culture that surrounds us we unconsciously absorb the value which our society places on parenting. The media, government funding, legislation and the prioritisation of support tells us the regard which our society holds for a parent's role.

Since its inception by British economists James Meade and Richard Stone, gross domestic product (GDP) has become the accepted formulation by which a nation's economy is assessed. In their formula, Meade and Stone focused almost entirely on the value of goods and services that were bought and sold in a country, and excluded all non-paid and non-traded work – most of which is carried out by women.

This oversight continued despite the protestations of several feminist economists, who pointed out the inappropriateness of such as system, particularly in

African countries where a population's very existence depended on long hours of work – cooking, cleaning, childcare, collecting water and gathering firewood – mostly carried out by women. Although some changes have been made over the years to how GDP is calculated, this non-traded work is still not included.

When a society properly recognises the existence of values other than material wealth, they become an accepted and integrated aspect of its systems. Approaches to education, finance, employment legislation, and even commerce can start to assume more spiritual values when we remind ourselves of parenting's importance as a matter of ultimate concern, and we begin to reinstate it as perhaps *the* most important role of any society.

There are many times in a parent's life that we might wish our more ideal selves to step in and act as role models for our children. Every hour, every conversation, every interaction wires their brain for their future selves. But authenticity is a more useful lesson for our children than attempting perfection.

Our job is to try to give them a coherent set of beliefs, where what they experience in family life is congruent with what we teach. This can and in fact should include dealing with suffering and falling short of our ideals. We want to equip our children with values which might guide them through the transparency of the materialistic world they live in, which can later develop into their own arrived at version of a moral code and conscience.

In a youth culture that reinforces focus on the self, we have to teach children to also learn self-transcendence. We want them to have fun, enjoy life and be happy, but also to know the silent joys of meaning and fulfilment. We want them to be able to move comfortably between world views, from the immediate and material, to the gestalt, the universal and the divine – to the risk of acknowledging mystery. We want them, and ourselves, to ultimately learn to blend the two ways of seeing, so that everything we see is seen through the eyes of the eternal. We want them to find their (w)holiness – their own, not ours – and their place in the whole of creation. We want them to feel big enough to fill the shoes of their place in the world, and yet small enough to experience awe. We want them to know, feel and practise compassion, so that they might recognise love to be far more than just an emotion. Because love may just turn out to be one of the fundamental energies of our planet.

'Some day, after harnessing the winds, the waves, the tides and gravity, We will harness for God the energies of love. And then, for a second time in the history of the world, Man will have discovered fire.'
– Pierre Teilhard de Chardin

As we have seen in Chapter 6, agape (originally from the Greek word 'agapé') is the highest type of love there is – unconditional love. Unlike the other types of love, romantic love and love of our family and friends, agape is love of what we may not like. As such it is an act of will – and a big ask. But that is what is demanded of us in the spiritual teachings of all traditions and it is agape, not love of the soft and fluffy type, which will create a more peaceful future for our children and lead to the evolution of humanity. Anything else is just kidding ourselves.

Agape is the heavy weight-lifting of love. It is developed, much like a muscle, by repeated and consistent practise over our and our children's life-times. Patience, generosity and forgiveness are perhaps the pillars that we all struggle with most. It is easy to give something we don't value to someone, or to be generous to those we like. But it is a much higher demand on us to be generous with our love and our forgiveness to someone we don't like, or who has hurt us.

This is where the difference between liking and loving comes in. Acting in love, or agape, means showing kindness, forgiveness or patience when we don't want to. To do this, we need to be able to see the divinity of the person behind the behaviour or personality that irritates us – or at least that they are also human beings who hope to avoid suffering. Whether or not society evolves to higher levels of agape depends on what each of us teaches our children today, tomorrow and the next day.

The stillness learned in our vertical plane of meditation can be a huge help for us and our children in developing enough self-awareness to stop ourselves saying something that hurts. Simply saying 'I have to move away before I say something I don't mean' is a demonstration of self-control that our children can learn from. Doing this in the middle of an argument is also an act of active love – real-life, un-glossy love. It is as much a prayer as any recited one. In these moments we can also open up our spiritual lexicon by saying that we are wounded or hurt, when we would prefer to say something that takes the attention off ourselves and attacks right back.

If someone says something that hurts, we can explain to the children that it wasn't a loving thing to say, differentiating between the person and what was said. We might differentiate between feelings of contentment (of the soul) and happiness (of the mind). We can help our children to differentiate between what we want and what we yearn for, the first a psychological attachment, the latter a pull of the soul.

When our children need to make difficult choices, or are thinking about how they responded to a situation, we can help them to feel the right answer: does one response or choice draw them upwards to a better version of themselves, and another pull them down or stagnate them? Does their choice come from a place of fear, of covering their back? Of saving face or personal risk reduction? Or does their choice come from a place of knowing that they are loved unconditionally, that they have a place in the universe that is only meant for them, that no matter what happens, their core is of love and remains as unmoveable as a rock? How might introducing them to the triad of the true, the good and the beautiful affect their decision?

Remember that as parents we have a foot in two separate generations, one of our upbringing and one of our parenthood. Our children's spiritual education is our responsibility, but our role is to help them to discover their own spiritual nature and path, not to offload ours. Their spiritual vocabulary may well be different to ours. That doesn't matter. Our job is to give our children and our partner licence to speak of spiritual matters, to give recognition to the fact that we all have a spiritual nature, a noetic inner voice.

It can be useful to add phrases such as 'stop and think for a moment about …' or 'don't answer me immediately but check in with yourself about …'. These types of phrases teach the child about the importance of listening to the small, still voice inside them, the vertical plane of the Seven-Day Soul, in a very practical way. But we have to do it too to make it a value they bring with them into adulthood.

It is not necessary to schedule special time to attend

to our family's noetic needs. Because the spiritual life is self-transcendent, it includes and surpasses the physical and mental self. It is the ground on which they exist. Imagine the wooden dolls traditional in Russian crafts, where one large wooden doll holds several, smaller ones, each doll nested within a larger one. Our spiritual self would be the outer, largest wooden doll that includes and holds all the others. So every physical and mental event can be looked at from a spiritual perspective because it is nested in the larger doll of our spiritual nature.

This was something that Phyllis, a client, discovered when business was going badly.

My husband had taken over the family business over twenty years ago. It was always hard work, but for the most part it ticked along okay. But more recently we were fighting a losing battle against cheaper international competitors, and we eventually knew we just couldn't keep the business going. We tried until the very end, even when we were almost making no money ourselves, because we couldn't face making people we employed redundant.

That was our way of practising our spiritual beliefs and showing kindness. I think that was self-transcendent. But when the family business did close, my husband used to go over and over its history, and his terrible sense of loss and letting down the family.

It was one day when we were talking about the past, and I was trying to get my husband to focus on the future, that I began to notice the different lenses on our problem that I had learned. This more universal, bird's eye view of the whole history of the business, the past and the lost future made me realise that no matter who was running the business, it would not have been able to compete with foreign suppliers, and someone was going to have to close it down. By my husband taking this terrible burden on himself, he had probably spared one of the children having to do it when they were older – perhaps with young children.

This perspective was such a new way of looking at the closure. It really helped my husband to find some meaning in the suffering; some goodness, but definitely not beauty, in the loss. He had shouldered a burden with dignity and kindness towards his employees, and also protected our kids from the suffering. It wasn't easy, but he had really handled it bravely and with generosity of effort when he had nothing else to give. It had in fact been an act of love.

The practicalities of everyday life give us endless opportunities to practise agape and the seven pillars. Our children learn to transcend their own egos when we show empathy for competition contestants on

TV shows. When kids see those who lose or make mistakes in reality shows, they learn to see the world from someone else's perspective.

Children experience awe when you encourage them to look up at the moon that we take so much for granted, or when we stare in appreciation of a view or piece of art. Help them to find out what fills them with awe. Perhaps it is the ball skills of a famous footballer, or the workmanship of a glamorous dress or expensive car. Don't worry if this feels very materialistic to you. The important thing is that you give them the vocabulary to recognise awe within themselves. And that they learn to use the word and connect it to a feeling of being taken out of self-consciousness, transfixed by something outside of themselves.

Humour is probably one of the greatest human connectors. Many people may be surprised at the prioritisation of humour as one of the seven pillars of the spiritual life. Far too often, humour is considered something that is somehow inferior to living a spiritual life, as if laughter is opposite to the very serious business of enlightenment. Of course we all differ in our taste in humour and the degree of humour we feel at home with. But humour is like a God-given escape hatch that helps us to shift perspective when we need to change lens. Seeing the funny side of something is nature's balm, a way of helping us to connect with someone which can instantly lift our spirit. It can give us a break from deep emotional hurt by lifting us up temporarily, and even has proven physiological healing benefits in the body.

Joy thrives in the absence of fear, so the more our faith or spiritual view of the world deepens into love, the less fearful we become. When we lose our deepest fear of being disconnected from the world, of being unloved or unwanted, we become emotionally freed to experience levity and joy. Humour creates joy.

Just remember there is nothing less funny than forced humour. You don't need to aim for a full belly laugh nor research pithy one-liners. Sometimes simply helping your child (and your spouse) to notice which of their friends lift their spirits and which sap their energies is a useful life tool to help them manage their spiritual energy budget. Most of us have people who rely on us, or who may even take much of our energy. If we give it willingly and consciously as part of our giving to the world, then this is perfectly fine.

But sometimes we can spend a lifetime having our energies taken from us because we spend our spare hours with the same people out of habit. If you can teach your child an awareness of their spiritual energy, then they can learn to make sure that they replenish themselves, as well as giving. We need people around us who support us, lift us, stand beside us, who pull us up, who listen to us, advise us and show interest in our opinions. We need people who make us laugh and people who hear us cry. Our spiritual re-fulfilment may come from our higher power directly, or through the company of others.

Sitting with a child in an armchair imagining your heads and hearts being filled with love from above, and then seeing this love streaming out of your toes (like a never-ending flow through a tap), or streaming out of your mouth (kind words), or fingertips (kind deeds) is a fun way to introduce the notion of spiritual energy to a child. You can extend the practise by asking your child to see if it is possible to imagine leaving the tap open at the top and turned on all day, so that love continuously flows through them. It becomes a powerful metaphor that the oldest and the youngest of us can use whenever we need some extra patience or strength. And all without ever mentioning the word 'prayer' or 'religion' if you think this might send them running.

Don't get stuck on the idea of night-time prayers if your child is pulling away from them. If this is a practise you have carried out with your children since they were small, it can be a bit heartbreaking when they just won't engage or even point-blank refuse. Again, move away from ideas of how prayer should be done, and help them to find their own way. It may not be a case of pure laziness, as much as a loss of any connection to the language you are using or the unconscious version of a God that answers requests that turns them off.

You might try suggesting that your child takes a leaf out of the prayer books of the monks who bookended their day with a review of that day, the times they practised love and where they could have acted more lovingly. If they really aren't interested in shaping this into any form of prayer, then try introducing it (lightly does it) as a conversation over dinner or in the car. Even a slight nod to a sense of review and learning will do, with phrases such as 'what does your conscience tell you?' or 'with the benefit of hindsight, what would have been a better way to respond to that situation?' With this one, less is definitely more – you want your children to be able to talk to you without feeling like you are going to make them acutely aware that they may not have acted as they should have. A quick throwaway phrase about yourself can be the easiest way to do this. 'In my heart of hearts I know I should have...' is a strong but subtle lesson in conscience. If you habitually sprinkle words such as 'love', 'heart' and 'soul' into your everyday language, these conversations and phrases will seem less jarring and easier to carry out.

Giving our children a spiritual education means educating them towards the ultimate meaning of their lives, the largest context in which they live, their innate universal or divine nature, and the immutability of their place in the world. As young adults, many of them will be attracted by the ideas of various different world traditions, and educating themselves in this way can only be a positive thing. But ultimately, all wisdom traditions make demands upon us, demands for personal responsibility in what we do, and practises aimed to ensure our spiritual development. No matter what tradition we might use to arrive at an understanding of ultimate truth, the path is one of action as well as 'thinking about'.

This sense of conscientious responsibility towards God or ultimate truth is gently nurtured in the day-to-day life of the ministry of family. Existential spirituality is always about relationship. If God, ultimate reality or our higher power is not a being in the sky, but Being itself, then the only way to be with God, is in how we 'be' in relation to others. If we can teach our children this, then we have done enough.

> **'The secret to inner peace lies in understanding our inner core values – those things in our lives that are most important to us – and then seeing that they are reflected in the daily events of our lives.'**
>
> **– From *What Matters Most*
> by Hyrann W. Smith**

10

Further, Higher, Deeper

PIL (Purpose In Life) Not Pills

'He who has a why to live for can bear almost
any how'

– Friedrich Nietzsche

They say happiness walks on busy feet. In modern life
we are not short of things to busy us. Experts tell us how
to clean our homes, improve fitness, eat well, raise our
children, find a partner, get a better job, stay married,
and so on. Yet despite our packed schedules, many of
us continue to feel that something is missing. Could
it be that we're stuffing an ever-increasing amount of
information and material goods into the gaps of our
lives, in the hope that this 'stuff' will make us happier?

To a small and short-lived extent, this over-stuffing
behaviour does indeed make us feel happier. However,
research shows that very soon after we buy ourselves
that item that we thought we wanted, a process called
'hedonic adaptation' is activated within us. Hedonic

adaptation means that after a short period of time, our levels of happiness revert back to where they were before the purchase, to hover close to a sort of predetermined set point. In fact, with research now showing that 50 per cent of our level of happiness is determined by genetics, it is quite difficult to move our happiness levels upwards without some effort on our part, in what and how we do things. The good news is that wellbeing is much more than happiness alone, and that there is more than one type of happiness. Reaching it requires a full flourishing of our being, as we are and as we can be.

Through mindfulness, an increasing number of people have become at least a little familiar with Buddhist teachings on learning to live in the now, and this has been incredibly useful for the mentally absent Western mind. But mindfulness is just a small piece of Buddhist thought; it cannot fulfil us completely. As some writers have noted, we are not human beings, but human 'becomings'. Human beings are always in a dynamic state of flux – a movement of growth towards the future.

Growing Further, Higher, Deeper

If you were to once again draw your life as a line on a sheet of paper, you would see the many directions in which we can grow. In getting to know, and show the world, our authentic selves, we can grow more depth. In discovering or creating a purpose in life for ourselves, we can reach and grow in extension, creating a sense of pull towards a personally relevant path in life. When we push ourselves to be the best we can be, striving to achieve our potential, we grow in height.

These potential growth directions create the expanse of our lives: the larger context that gives us a sense of meaning. While our further, higher, deeper dimensions are distinct from each other – some looking inward to the development of the self, others aiming outwards in the service of others – growth in any of them can bring us a sense of meaning.

Being True to Ourselves

Philosopher Søren Kierkegaard once quipped that on entering the gates of heaven, we will not be asked why we were not more like a saint, but why we were not more of ourselves. The ancient roman philosopher and statesman Seneca would have approved. Seneca described the happy life as one that was conducive to one's own nature. Since then, thousands of writers have followed this line of thought. Two of the best-known examples are Shakespeare's 'To thine own self be true', and Socrates' 'To know thyself is the beginning of wisdom'. These writers and philosophers did not mean to recommend that we should merely be more 'us', but that we should work to evolve the way we can best contribute to the evolution of the world.

'Be yourself; everybody else is already taken.'
– Oscar Wilde

As positive psychology (the study of what makes us happy) has matured, we've begun to see that trying to be perpetually happy, in the literal sense of the word – constantly laughing, smiling and being cheerful – is a fruitless, short-sighted exercise. Rather than naïvely trying to ignore the existence of suffering in the world, barricading ourselves against any sadness that might come our way, we can instead learn to live – and even grow – through the challenging events of our lives. Learning to get through these episodes of suffering helps us to grow more resilient.

Terms such as 'resilience' and 'grit' have been around a long time in business literature, but neither captures the idea of fully recognising how self-understanding can help a person to not only survive difficult life events, but to find these events meaningful. Sigmund Freud believed that as a civilisation, we all need to stop living our lives in service of ourselves and our most basic drives for pleasure and the easy life, and instead start living for the greater good. Our purpose in life, according to Freud, is to serve our nature's better angels, and the world beyond ourselves.

·····················On Reflection·····················

Perceiving the greater meaning of difficulties in life can be a struggle when we are in the midst of the suffering. But see if it is possible for you to look back at a difficult time to discern what you might have learned or gained from the experience. Perhaps your suffering sheltered someone else from shouldering the burden, or made you become more compassionate towards others who suffer the same way. Take a few moments to reflect on whether you might also have expanded your life line in a particular dimension, of height, depth, or forwards towards your life's purpose or purposes.

'This is the true joy in life, the being used for a purpose recognised by yourself as a mighty one.'
– George Bernard Shaw

Dostoyevski's version of happiness is fulfilling the purpose of our lives, but many people aren't quite sure what that purpose is. Is it something we choose to create ourselves? Or do we find purpose, or does it find us? Is it something we happen to like doing, which we then retro-fit, in order to believe that it was always the pre-determined purpose of our lives? Do we have lots of purposes in life?

The answers to these questions are different for everyone, but those with a belief in a personal god or a higher power are more likely to see a role carved out for them for their time on earth. 'To be religious,' as Albert Einstein put it, 'is to have found an answer to the question, "What is the meaning of life?".' But everyone of us, believers and non-believers alike, are equally capable of finding a personal purpose on earth, whether it is immediately clear to us or not.

Each of us is an irreplaceable piece in the jigsaw of human history, because of the uniqueness of our time, our nature, and our intersections with other lives; the space that we inhabit. That space is often unnoticed by us as we look outward from it. Often it is only at the passing of those we have loved that we see the spaces they leave empty behind them. Similarly, we are each the keepers of a unique fingerprint in space and time.

Height Psychology: Striving To Be Our Best Selves

Homeostasis is the natural tendency of the body towards balance, which was first discovered by Walter Cannon when he was studying the biology of the stress response. When we feel out of kilter through mental or physical stress, our body will attempt to redress the imbalance of neurotransmitters and hormones flooding our system by setting off a counter-balancing set of chemicals to bring our physiology back in to equilibrium. Huge academic praise and accolades were heaped on Cannon by the scientific community for his research, which focused on the workings of the adrenal glands, and their now famous hormone adrenaline, which gave us the modern phrases 'adrenaline junkie', and 'adrenalin high'. Most of us will have experienced the often unwelcome effects of adrenaline in our bodies at times of stress, such as 'jelly legs' or a racing heart rate. At times like these, what we desperately want most is to be able to return ourselves to the balance of homeostasis.

In the workplace, workers strive to achieve work–life balance as if work is separate to life and we must pour ourselves equal measures of both. But balance is only one part of the picture of who we are, only one aspect of wellbeing. What we also need to stay healthy is a sense of growth: a dynamic, moving stretch of ourselves towards something more than we are now.

Hans Selye, an Austro-Hungarian endocrinologist and contemporary of Walter Cannon, was the first person to introduce the word 'stress' into the common vernacular. Selye identified two different types of stress, calling positive stressors 'eustress' (based on the Greek word 'eu' meaning good, similar to Aristotle's 'eudaimonia'), and negative stressors, 'distress'. The latter term is what most of us mean when we use the word 'stress' today.

Selye's work packed a big punch in terms of its impact on modern medicine because it was the first scientific link between stress and disease. But Selye also saw how his work on eustress and distress related to the far larger context of finding our purpose and meaning in life.

Each of us, according to Selye, has a finite amount of what he called 'adaptation energy'. This is the energy we can expend on stressors, good or bad. The amount of adaptation energy that each of us has is determined by our heredity. Once it is spent, it can be superficially replaced by, for example, a good night's sleep or a holiday; but it can never really be fully replenished, and will ultimately be depleted in old age.

What was really interesting in Selye's work was the biological and endocrine explanation he offered to the psychology of meaning. Not only do the stresses of everyday life use up some of our adaptation energies, but these energies need to be spent for us to satisfy our innate need for self-expression. The stress of fulfilling work, and the distress of frustration or lack of work, can both use up our adaptation energy, but the distress of a lack of fulfilment is far more likely to lead to disease. Selye wasn't suggesting that we don't need some sense of balance in the body: after exercising we need to rest, after a long day at work we need to put our feet up. What he was saying was that alongside this re-balancing that the body does to help us to regain some biological homeostasis, we also have a biological need for personal fulfilment in whatever role our innate tastes take us. Just as blocking our need for sleep or food will eventually lead to illness, blocking our built-in need for personal fulfilment will also lead to disease.

'It is the hunger for achievement that brings joie de vivre.'

– Hans Selye

When Sigmund Freud was asked what makes us happy, his answer was simple: work and love. Selye was of the same view. Here were two world experts in the fields of psychology and medicine saying that we have an active role to play in the world, that we are not seated passengers in the passage of time but biologically programmed to participate in its evolution.

Selye saw work as a biological necessity for personal wellbeing and not just a means to an end. For him, the need to work, construct and alter our environment was a law of nature; our task is to find the work that satisfies us and hurts no one. It can be the work of building ourselves by self-improvement, or work in the service of some greater good. But to be fulfilling, the work has to be personally meaningful, in line with our talents and tastes. This doesn't mean that we can avoid stress even when we love our work, but that this type of more positive stress is using our adaptation energies in the way they should be spent in our lifetime. Stress, Selye said, is in all types of work, but distress is not.

·················On Reflection·················

Tasked with Life

When we are rushing from one task to the next, thinking about whether those tasks are eustress or distress can be the last thing on our mind. But if you take today as an example, see if it is possible for you to list the various tasks of your day as either providing eustress or distress. Some might contain a little – or a lot – of both. Studying for an exam might be immediately distressing, but also offer you the obvious long-term benefits of self-improvement and personal growth. Other jobs, like taking out the bins, might seem just repetitive and dull. In your diary will be things that drain you and things that nourish you. See if you can label them and schedule your day to manage your adaptation energies better. If you know that your energy dips after 4pm, schedule in a eustress task or something that has personal meaning for you. So often, we just make a to-do list and then go through it without any logic to the order. Learning to schedule our day appropriately wakes us up to the inherent nourishment that is available to us in the seven days of each week.

There may be things on your list that you habitually dread but which, with new insight, can be seen as moving you towards your life's purpose. For example, during my early childhood, bath time was probably a bit of a drudge for my mother. Yet one of my fondest childhood memories is of being wrapped up in a warm towel and dusted in talcum powder. I used to run down the stairs to see how many powdery footprints I could make before the powder was gone.

Sometimes we need to remember that in distress, or even the seeming irrelevance of repetitive tasks, we are building someone else's happiness, and lifelong gratitude.

For many of us, below the biological and psychological explanations of our need to strive for growth and fulfilment is the original source of our motivation: a spiritual need for movement towards the full flourishing of our being. We are not designed to be static. Just as the fibres of a muscle are torn in exercise, only to regrow larger and stronger when they repair, we too need to have experiences that push us, that cause tensions in us, in order for us to grow. It is this growth that provides us with our sense of place and purpose in the world. We work to look after our children (purpose) because we love them (meaning). Or, we work hard at our jobs because we need the money (purpose), because we want to provide for those we love (meaning). Similarly, the athlete trains hard to take ten seconds off his/her personal best (purpose) because s/he will win the tournament (social context), but also feel a sense of mastery and achievement (meaning).

Writing in 1974, Selye warned that the continuous cutting back of work hours that was happening as people were being replaced by machines was going to lead to a point where work deprivation would be society's biggest problem. Where people are left with no way to fulfil their need for accomplishment, they often become destructive to themselves and others. Isn't it ironic that again today, nearly fifty years later, we are facing the same problem in zero-hour contracts, and employees being laid off work due to the introduction of electronic banking, online selling and artificial intelligence?

What was needed then, and is still needed today, is for society as a group to review its mental map of what progress is and how it should be defined. What do we mean by 'onwards' and 'forwards'? To whom or what should progress be the servant? Will it be in the service of capitalism, socialism, the West, the nation, the individual, the world, the poor, technology, or any one particular value system?

It can be difficult to objectively perceive the value system of our society. Values feel like givens as opposed to 'chosens', which we might opt in and out of. Should future progress, as Selye suggests, be in teaching 'play professions' – teaching arts, philosophy, crafts and science to the public in order to fill the noetic void left by lack of meaningful work? There is no limit, according to Selye, to how much human beings can work on the perfection of their own selves.

The variation in the collective values of a nation were

perfectly encapsulated in the inauguration speeches of two presidents of America:

> **'Ask not what your country can do for you –**
> **ask what you can do for your country.'**
> **– President John F. Kennedy,**
> **Inaugural Address, January, 1961**

> **'A nation exists to serve its citizens.'**
> **– President Donald J. Trump,**
> **Inaugural Address, January, 2017**

Finding Eudaimonic Contentment and Your Authentic Self

On Reflection

Think back to eulogies that you've heard at funerals. Each eulogy highlighted the particular characteristics of the individual being laid to rest. Now take a moment to consider the legacy you want to leave to the world, your family or loved ones. What are the things that you want to be remembered for?

As you do this exercise, be true to what you would really like to be remembered for, rather than strengths that you feel you should have. What aspects of yourself have you been praised for in the past? What do you know to be your strengths? If you were asked to write a 'how to' manual, what would be the topic you would most easily write about?

What skills seem to come easier to you than to other people? Are there people who already do, or who might in the future, benefit from your knowledge and expertise? If you were an agony aunt, what problems do you think you could help people with most? If you were to wake up famous tomorrow morning, what is the thing you are most likely to be famous for?

These are all questions that can help you to find your innate strengths. Take some time with these questions, and see if you can see a theme emerging in your answers.

You may find that it is not so much knowledge as character strengths that make themselves apparent to you; strengths such as faithfulness, loyalty, persuasiveness, justice, fairness, energy, friendliness, encouragement, leadership, listening, charisma, gentleness and courage. Keep your answers near to hand, or write them out somewhere you will see them regularly.

These are hints towards your role in this life, the tools you have been given to carve out your space. Over the coming days, see where you can build these parts of yourself into your day, repeatedly reorienting your activities towards your strengths. Don't worry if you don't arrive at some clear image or label for your purpose in life. As we have learned from so many researchers and philosophers, our purpose is mostly in the 'how' of what we do, not the form.

What Makes Us Happy?

Hedonism is a term that most of us would associate with excesses of physical and material pleasures focused on the self. But hedonic happiness, the type that allows us to enjoy physical pleasures, materialism, living for the moment, and comfort, is not completely at odds with real happiness. We just need to temper our natural taste for immediate gratification and comfort with the longer-lasting benefits of eudaimonia, a more spiritual happiness.

They are not opposites of each other. Hedonism comes from the more ancient part of the brain, where our instincts for survival, pleasure and avoidance of pain reside. Eudaimonia, on the other hand, requires the higher functioning of the human brain, which allows us to see past the present moment, to overcome our mere survival instincts, to empathise with others, to contemplate our legacy, and to see life through a larger lens.

Small bursts of hedonism of the more gentle kind will help us to keep moving on the path of our life purpose. But we must remember that our life's purpose is about how we live the seven days of each week, rather than some vague idea of our ideal self in the future. It is about how we interact with the next person we meet or speak with. And nature, in its wisdom, has designed happiness to be deeply intertwined with these opportunities for social connection.

The Purpose of Relationships

The longest known study of longevity and wellbeing, carried out by Harvard University since 1938, shows that strong social connection not only makes us happier, but also makes us healthier in brain and body. Having good relationships, where there is trust and the freedom to be ourselves, is the single greatest indicator of happiness, health and wellbeing. It is not about the number of people we know, nor the amount of times we go out socialising, but about the quality of those relationships, the support they provide us, and the trust within them.

Our sense of purpose, then, must incorporate building more of these relationships, which nurture not only ourselves, but also the other person within the relationship. Love turns out to be knit into the very fabric of our existence, warming and rewarding us, pushing us on to ever-increasing acts of greater love. It is our failure to grasp this fundamental aspect of human design which causes feelings of purposelessness and an existential void.

Purpose Anxiety

The pressure to find a single and unique purpose or meaning in life has led to a phenomenon known as 'purpose anxiety'. Mark Twain famously wrote that the two most important days in our life are the day we are born and the day we find out why. These are poetic but loaded words. They suggest that there exists a preordained purpose for each of us, one that is stable and unique. But research shows that purpose and meaning can be found in many ways that are personal but not necessarily unique to us. Because what we consider to be meaningful depends to a large extent on our attributions and appraisals, our purpose(s) can be discovered retrospectively, when we look back at an event in our lives and see it in relation to how our life evolved, how it connected us to the things we value and that which is meaningful in our lives.

> **'Life can only be understood backwards;**
> **but it must be lived forwards.'**
> **– Søren Kierkegaard, Philosopher**

Finding our purpose is a reaching forwards in extension, rather than the wider context sense of the breadth of life's meaning, but certainly understanding what gives our life meaning will also give us clues to its purpose. Discovering purpose demands that we pay attention to our values in life, because it is these values that will help our life to make sense. Purpose is by nature teleological, that aspect that draws us forward in our evolution, or for the religious, on our path towards whatever we consider the divine. Trying to find one single purpose in our lives, or believing that if we have found it in one job we will not find it in another, is likely to set us up for disappointment.

Love is the ultimate 'how', the all-encompassing final purpose of our lives. Not all of us will arrive at a clear sense of our 'job' in the world, perhaps because many people mistakenly presume that their role must be unique to them. When we remind ourselves that purpose is not so much about what we will do in our lives, but about how we will live our lives, we can let go of our expectation that our job title will give us purpose, and instead bring a sense of purpose to everything we do. Through the seven pillars of gratitude, generosity, forgiveness, patience, awe, humour and stillness, each of us can stand over the part we play in life, with each pillar acting as our purpose in a given day. It is not enough for us to say we believe in ideals such as world peace, ending poverty, and so on. We must all shake off our inertia and take up our personal responsibility. Sometimes, however, our purpose is to care for someone much closer to hand who needs our loving attention. We can only play our part in the world if we stay on stage, playing the role we have been given. By paying attention to those aspects of ourselves that feel true, that feel good and of virtue, we can find the role by which we will deliver our lines in the play of humankind's evolution. No matter how apparently humble our role, we have the choice to speak the lines of love.

·················On Reflection··················

Present Purpose

No matter how good our intentions are at the start of the day, it is human nature to revert quickly to the unconsciousness of habit, and how we did things yesterday. Take this moment – whether you are at the airport, in a coffee shop, or curled up in a chair at home – to ask yourself, what is my purpose for the rest of the day? With this, I'm not talking about your to-do list, but your how-will-I-do list. What is society, personal responsibility, or your higher power asking of you for the rest of your day? And for the days to come? What do you ask of yourself? How might you be a better version of yourself? Bringing your understanding of the purpose of your life into the here and now puts the reins of control right back in your hands. If you are spiritual, you might choose to ask a divine power what it is that is asked of you today. But whether our view on the world is spiritual or not, every one of us would benefit from repeatedly tuning in to the moment, to ask the purpose of every hour of our lives, so that we may use it well. Your purpose this hour may be to put extra effort into cooking a nourishing meal for the family, to stop at the desk of a colleague to lift their spirits, or to look after your own health by getting some down time. Perhaps your purpose right now is to choose a book that enriches your knowledge and lets you see the world through someone else's eyes; or maybe it's to add an extra line of thanks in your email, highlighting the effort someone has put into their work. Purpose does not so much need to be created by us, so much as it needs to be seen.

Reaching For Health

Since the development of techniques to measure a person's purpose in life (PIL), research has shown it to have multiple health benefits. Findings in the study of PIL have repeatedly shown a link between purpose in life and longevity in all ages, and a decreased risk of mortality in older adults. PIL helps us to sleep better, and results in a lower rate of sleep disorders.

It is neuro-protective in that it helps to preserve a healthy brain and decreases the likelihood of developing mild cognitive impairment – even in people whose later autopsy showed that Alzheimer's plaques were present in their brain. This means that people with a high sense of PIL seem to be able to withstand a higher rate of brain injury before developing symptoms of Alzheimer's disease.

PIL has been linked to a 72 per cent lower risk of death by stroke and a 44 per cent lower rate of death from cardiovascular disease, in addition to increased levels of good cholesterols, reduced levels of disease-causing inflammation in the body, and a slower rate of the build-up of inflammation that normally occurs when we experience one stressor after another.

Related research from the US found that people who reported having had more experiences of hedonic happiness in their lives had higher levels of pro-inflammatory genes (which cause damaging inflammation) in their blood than those whose wellbeing came from a eudaimonic type of happiness. While this type of study can't show us a direct cause and effect (it may be that living a life of eat, drink and be merry style hedonism includes foods and experiences that cause inflammation), it might be that when we find eudaimonic happiness we need less sources of hedonic happiness.

It seems to be that in the grand design of life, we are meant to utilise our talents and strengths in outward service; and that in doing this, we spend our life's energies on the building of our common home. There is no other person on the planet who will meet the same people as you do today; who will come to them in the same role, with the same panoply of personality traits and strengths, at the same moment in time. Yours is a unique role. Play it well.

··············On Reflection··············

Sometimes our purpose can seem very far away from where we are today. But this is a mistaken view of our purpose in life. You don't necessarily need to change your job, partner or the country you live in to find your purpose and the beneficial effects of the deep-seated happiness of eudaimonia. Here is a list of some 'purposes' you might choose to utilise right away – you will notice that none of them are job titles. As you read through them, circle the words that feel familiar to you, those that you believe are part of who you are. Other words might spring to mind as you go through the list. Write them down and circle them as your personal strengths. When you have done this, take the circled list and put it somewhere you will see regularly. These words will become the purpose of your day.

I am here to do what I do . . .

Patiently	Deliberately
Repeatedly	Doggedly
Tidily	Sharply
Cooperatively	Speedily
Comically	Swiftly
Intuitively	Inquisitively
Gently	Fiercely
Guidingly	Daringly
Insistently	Seriously

Persistently	Openly
Courageously	Majestically
Publicly	Modestly
Vociferously	Powerfully
Encouragingly	Politely
Bravely	Neatly
Diligently	Generously
Cautiously	Cheerfully
Eagerly	Bravely
Honestly	Faithfully
Tenderly	Warmly
Noisily	Manually
Safely	Justly
Beautifully	Artistically
Calmly	Obediently
Precisely	Frankly
Naturally	Elegantly
Cleverly	Wisely
Efficiently	Energisingly
Cost-effectively	Technically

When we begin to see the huge responsibilities put to us every day, everything we do becomes powered with possibility and purpose.

11
Inhaling the Breadth
of Meaning

'Love is our true destiny. We do not find
the meaning of life by ourselves alone
– we find it with another.'

– Thomas Merton

Have you ever hit a white snooker ball into the triangle
of coloured balls and watched them move out across
the table in all directions, carried by the energy received
from the white ball? That is what we do every day.

So much of how we feel, think and then behave is
primed by our interactions with others: we take on
their energy and bring it with us as we go through
our day, passing that energy on to everyone we meet
without any conscious awareness of what it is that
we are passing on. Anyone who has ever dieted will
be familiar with the phrases 'I'm having a good day'
or 'I'm having a bad day', meaning that we've either
eaten healthily today or not so well. While the phrases

have differing meanings, inherent in both is the idea that the day is happening to us – that we have no say in the matter and are mere onlookers, waiting to see what will be sent our way on the conveyor belt of life.

We must not allow ourselves to take this attitude when it comes to finding meaning in our lives. The seven pillars of the Seven-Day Soul are our personal daily mission statements, our way of saying that we accept our responsibility to be fully awake to what we put out into the world, that we understand we are always making an impact on the world, good or bad, and that we are willing to put work into designing a life that benefits not only ourselves, but the people around us too.

The Choice of Responsibility

Responsibility for the meaning of our life was a fundamental teaching of Viennese psychiatrist Viktor Frankl. Frankl was a young ambitious Jewish psychiatrist in Vienna when the Second World War broke out. In 1940 he took up the position of head of the neurological department of a hospital for Jewish people in Vienna. The following year, he married his first wife, Tilly.

It was the same year that the SS carried out their first gassing experiments in Auschwitz. Frankl had been granted a work permit for America which would have offered him and his wife safety, but he let it expire in an attempt to help his parents, feeling that the status of his job might offer them some protection from the

Nazis. This was not to be. On 25 September, 1942, when Frankl was thirty-seven years old, he, his wife and his parents were arrested and taken to Theresienstadt concentration camp in Bohemia. Frankl's father died there of starvation, in his son's arms. After two years, Frankl and his wife Tilly were moved to Auschwitz.

A week later, his mother also arrived in the camp and was immediately murdered in the gas chambers. Tilly was moved on to Bergen-Belsen, where she died, aged just twenty-four. Frankl was moved once again to Kaufering and then to Türkheim, both subsidiary camps of the infamous Dachau, from where he was eventually freed.

During his time in the camps, Frankl sometimes worked as a doctor to the other prisoners, helping where he could to protect them. Within the same horrific circumstances of camp life, he noticed the extremes of human responses, with some inmates colluding with the Nazis in acts of self-preservation, and others sharing their crumbs of food with other prisoners.

Throughout his imprisonment, Frankl set himself the task of rewriting a manuscript for a book he had begun to write before his arrest, but which had been taken from him. Writing on any slips of paper he could find, sometimes memorising his thoughts, he began to develop his ideas into a book that would eventually be published after his liberation. *Man's Search for Meaning* became one of the most famous books of the twentieth century.

'In the concentration camps, for example, in this living laboratory and on this testing ground, we watched and witnessed some of our comrades behave like swine while others behaved like saints. Man has both potentialities within himself; which one is actualized depends on decisions but not on conditions.'

— **Viktor Frankl,** *Man's Search for Meaning*

For Frankl, our being human means that we are responsible for our existence no matter what circumstances we find ourselves in, and we need to consciously choose what we are going to be rather than be driven by our more basic bodily instincts. Our existence needs to be intentional and directed outwards from ourselves towards something or someone other than ourselves. Here was a man who had suffered, and witnessed the torture, murder and slow dying of so many people around him; and yet he was able to say that even in these circumstances, we have a choice about how we will respond. He was not saying that we should suffer needlessly, but only that even in inescapable suffering, we still hold the freedom to choose our attitudes.

Frankl saw human beings as comprised of three inseparable dimensions: the biological, the psychological, and the noetic. For Frankl, the 'noos' (from which we get the term 'noetic' and 'noogenic') refers to that spiritual aspect of us that strives and yearns to become a better version of ourselves, whether or not we have religious beliefs. 'Noogenic' means anything that comes from this deepest part of our being. For Frankl, looking at humanity as being made up of just mind and body was like shining a torch on the end of a cylinder. This would cast a circular shadow on the wall behind, just as shining a torch on a coin would, but we would completely miss the full picture of the cylinder.

If, for example, you were to hold a cylindrical battery on its side and shine the torch on one end, it would cast a circular shadow on the wall behind, giving you no hint as to the depth of the cylinder. In the same way, said Frankl, when we ignore our noetic dimension, which encompasses the mind and body within it, we miss the fullest picture of ourselves.

It would be easy for us all to excuse ourselves from the demands of responsibility that this view puts on us. There is a strange tendency in our psychology to presume that lessons learned from these great acts of self-transcendence in the most extreme conditions don't really apply to the ordinariness of our own lives – that love practised in a concentration camp isn't possible in the home, office, hairdresser's, shop, factory, hospital or wherever we work.

But Frankl believed that the 'defiant power of the human spirit' has an innate need to strive towards fulfilling our potential to be who we can be, wherever we are; and that, just as in the Seven-Day Soul, we need to be looking at the opportunities that every moment offers us for meaning. Every moment is our 'summons', the call to find our 'monuments to meaning' in the situations of daily life, which allow us to transcend ourselves and the needs of our loved ones to include a wider circle of humanity. No one can find meaning for us; we must discover it for ourselves.

The Seven Pillars as Our Monuments to Meaning

Monuments, historical or otherwise, act as reminders of things that we hold to be of value. They can help us to remember lessons learned by past history, reorienting us to cherish or to change according to those lessons. The seven pillars of generosity, gratitude, forgiveness, patience, awe, humour and stillness can be our monuments to meaning in the day, particularly when we struggle to discover what is being asked of us in any one moment. These pillars are what we ask of ourselves, the values that we set as our compass and our summons.

Frankl suggested three ways that we can all find the meaning of the moment:

1. **In creativity:** doing creative works or deeds. Meaning can be found through the accomplishment or achievement of a creative task, be that work, a hobby or creative arts.

Creative here means the expression of ourselves to the world, but this doesn't have to mean the traditional idea of 'creative'. Our work can be creative if it allows us to offer something of ourselves in it, be that the way we manage the company's photocopying needs, our unique way of answering calls, or the way we cut a client's hair. These creative values help us to give to the world.

2. **By experiencing someone or something:** Meaning can be found when we stop to notice values such as goodness, beauty and truth through nature and culture; and by really experiencing another person in their uniqueness.

   How often do most of us pay attention to the unique, irreplaceability of the people we speak to during the day? How often are we still enough to really experience the camaraderie of the team, the quick wit of a colleague or the brilliance of a computer programme designed by a human mind?

3. **Through our attitude:** When faced with unavoidable pain, we can continue to find meaning in our lives through the attitude we bring to it, the stand we take. When we cannot change the situation, we have to change

ourselves. When we find meaning in suffering, it ceases to be suffering.

Freedom of attitude is taught in many spiritual traditions. Buddhist teachers compare inescapable suffering to being wounded by an arrow. If we ruminate and overly focus on our wound we add 'the second arrow of suffering'. Where might it be possible for you to become conscious of the attitude that has arrived with a disappointment, extra workload or some other stress? See if it is possible for you to consciously change your attitude, perhaps adopting your pillar for the day, as a means to jump-start your way out of habitual reactions. Is it possible to forgive someone who has snapped at you, or to be patient with someone who is taking their own stress out on you? Is it possible to feel grateful for the fact that you will eventually climb into a cosy bed even if you get home late, or to choose to act with dignity when someone else won't? Think about the ways you can ease the suffering of someone else in your work day, perhaps using your pillar of forgiveness. Freedom to choose our response gives us autonomy of attitude, even when a problem isn't within our control.

For Frankl, as for Hans Selye, the responsibility and freedom to choose to make our life our own, gives us a healthy tension, what he called a 'noõ-dynamic' stretching towards our potential. This means that we cannot use our eagerness to discover the ultimate meaning of life, the final explanation of everything, as a way of opting out of our responsibilities in the now. According to Frankl, it is not for us to ask the meaning of life, but instead to consider what life asks of us.

Lessons in Life

Mark was a 37-year-old father of three. He said that he was happily married, although he and his wife did sometimes have arguments about sharing the workload, and particularly the care of the children. Mark told me that he did his best when it came to staying fit – before having children, he had been very into fitness, and despite limitations on his time now that he was a father, he still tried to get out for a run at least once a week, and was careful of his alcohol intake.

Mark worked for an insurance company and liked it well enough. He loved his children and his wife, but said that he desperately missed having the time to do the voluntary work he used to do. As family life had became increasingly busy, he could no longer fulfil the hours required at the homeless shelter, and he'd had to step back from his role. He had tried to donate money to charity as a way to give when he couldn't give his time, but he felt that he had lost his feeling of really doing something good through volunteering. Life now just felt like the proverbial treadmill, and the future didn't look like being any different for many years to come. He said he knew he shouldn't complain; he recognised that he was lucky to have a job and a happy family, and he felt a bit greedy for wanting more – but he did want more. He described himself as not being depressed, just 'a bit down and kind of bored'.

Contributing to society, and the associated feelings of being of worth in the world, was a key value for Mark, as it is for many of us. But he showed an inflexibility in his definition of contribution. In his volunteering capacity in a homeless shelter, the results of his efforts were immediately visible. He didn't always get to speak with the people who attended the shelter – it depended on what job he was given to do. But he did always share in the sense of camaraderie and purpose available to him there.

Mark's pain was a type of soul pain – a feeling of loss of values and context for his living. Without being able to see the contribution he was making, his life felt a bit insipid. In conversation we talked about the ripple effects of the smallest of kind actions. We also explored the various ways in which he was contributing to society, such as by raising a family and being a good husband. These types of roles can seem to be very slow-burning, with their fruits taking a long time to ripen, and it takes some discipline to keep the end goal in view. But it is by repeatedly and intentionally choosing to see what we do in a larger context that we polish our spiritual lens on the world. On reflection, Mark felt that he could do a better job in his various current roles, so we began to map out ways he might do this over the coming weeks.

In the following session Mark reported that he had begun to 'wake up' more at home, to chat to the children more, and generally pay more attention to what was going on. Instead of simply explaining something in his son's homework, he had taken the time to find a video online that explained it better than he could.

At work, Mark stood up for someone who was being talked over, asked one more question about someone else's opinion before giving his own opinion where he could in a conversation, and consciously smiled more. He also noted that the family dog was from a rescue home and that this was another way in which he was contributing to a greater good.

Mark also attempted to measure, as we had discussed, the duration of the effects of a kindness done to him on his own mood and behaviour – for instance, when someone let him into a line of traffic, he found he was more likely to do the same for another person later. In this and subsequent conversations, Mark began to see the contributions his actions were already making to the world around him, and that these effects could be positive or negative depending on the choices he made. Being a truly conscious parent became his preferred way to make a difference, because he saw that his children not only responded to this, but it was also helping his marriage. He also felt that bringing up three kind and compassionate children would make an even bigger difference in the world than he could achieve alone. He began to take a fresh look at every aspect of his day-to-day life to see how he could do it better, or with more compassion.

Ample research supports the importance of a sense of control and autonomy in our lives for wellbeing. We get stressed when we feel we don't have the resources, knowledge, time, manpower or whatever might be needed to meet the demands of a task. But stress happens at both extremes – when we feel stretched too far beyond our abilities, or when we feel understretched, underutilised or unfulfilled. In the research, these noetic needs are usually spoken about in psychological terms – such as aspiration or motivation – because we don't feel comfortable enough to speak about our spiritual needs in public life. We treat the sick at the two levels of body and mind.

But Frankl believed that many of our so-called physical and psychological illnesses actually come from the noetic dimension of ourselves. Addictions, unsuccessful relationships, depression and anxiety can all come from a feeling of disconnectedness, a sense of being lost at sea in the world because we haven't been given the spiritual vocabulary to recognise our need for the wider, whole-making lens that places our life in relation to everything else. Without this noetic education, we are forced to try to resolve our illnesses at the levels of mind and body, treating the symptoms instead of the source.

Every now and then life gives us an opportunity to see more than the shadows cast on the wall, to see and feel that the whole of who we are is more than the bag of bones that some would have us think we are. We will never get out of our hall of mirrors in trying to understand ourselves if we do not understand that the physical and psychological aspects that we see are merely projections from the noetic core, from which we are projected in the first place. It isn't that we do not have these physical and psychological dimensions to us, but that these are lower aspects of ourselves, contained within our noological dimensions. As Frankl put it, *we are spirit and we have a body and mind*. Sure, if a doctor taps on just the right point on the knee, the lower leg will jerk outwards in an involuntary reflex. Our cycles of sleep, eating, immune and other chemical reactions carry on without our knowing.

The mind endlessly narrates the subtitles to life's events without our invitation, and impulses, drives and emotions will carry us some way through life like a driverless car. All of these are the vital workings of the mind and body. But really living life demands the input of our true self, the part of us that is truly unique and without blueprint. The part of us that not only reacts but also responds and interacts with the world in conscious and responsible choice.

This responsibility relies on us developing our conscience. For the non-religious person, conscience might be their inner voice; for the religious person, it might be the voice of God. But no matter how we imagine it to be, we need our conscience to keep us on track, steering us towards responsibility for our answer not to the meaning of life, but to what life asks of us.

'The man who regards his own life and that of his fellow creatures as meaningless is not merely unfortunate but almost disqualified for life.'
– Albert Einstein

Learned Meaninglessness

US researchers first wrote about the phenomenon of learned helplessness in the 1960s, when they noticed that dogs who were put in to a cage with a mild electrical charge going through the floor stopped looking for a part of the floor that was not electrified even when it became available to them. The animals seemed to presume that escape was impossible and beyond their control. The purpose of these rather cruel experiments was to suggest that humans too are susceptible to this learned lack of control over their lives after repeated setbacks, and that this might be a factor in depression.

The person who has applied for countless jobs without success may feel not only disheartened but also disenabled. The worker who puts enormous effort into their work, but receives no praise or reward, learns that their efforts to gain promotion are futile. The student who repeatedly fails their maths tests, despite trying very hard, learns that their efforts are have no bearing on their test outcomes, and soon gives up. There are many examples of instances in life where it can seem that our efforts are futile, that circumstances are not controllable and life appears meaninglessness. In *Man's Search for Meaning*, Viktor Frankl recounts:

> *The camp inmate was frightened of making decisions and of taking any sort of initiative whatsoever. This was the result of a strong feeling that fate was one's master, and that one must not try to influence it in any way, but instead to let it take its own course.*

This learned meaninglessness might be acquired in a very similar way by individuals in less extreme situations. If the family we grow up in, or the country we live in, fails to offer us ideas, hope or a way of seeing the world as whole, we have a much greater chance of falling at the first hurdle. But as Frankl's experiences showed, even in the worst of conditions, it is possible to surmount hopelessness, to reinstate meaning and self-agency, to control at least how we respond to the situations we find ourselves in. Meaning can be given to us through the culture we live in. But where it is not offered to us, we can find it for ourselves. If our homes and our culture do not instil this dimension of depth in our lives – placing all the things that we do in high relief against the larger backdrop of our spiritual development and societal contribution – then we will come to believe that what we do simply doesn't matter.

The good news is that we can learn to provide for ourselves what may not have been transmitted to us through our families or culture. Teachings on living in the now remind us not to lose the preciousness of the current moment; but the now of our lives needs both past and future to give it meaning. Imagine how much healthier we'd be, as individuals and as society, if our parents, teachers and culture – the sea we swim in – learned to provide us with this sense of connection to the meaning dimension of our lives, thereby allowing us to see the ultimate meaning of why we do what we do.

If we cannot see the meaning of the small things in our lives, valuing only grand and public gestures, then we are operating at a very low level of consciousness. When any activity is taken solely at face value, devoid of its larger worth, we risk lapsing into learned meaninglessness.

Without education and a cultural valuing of the noetic part of ourselves, those in distress are often forced to attempt to understand their suffering in purely psychological or physical terms. If our culture does not give recognition to the wisdom of the heart and our need for a sense of place on the map, then neither do we have the words to speak this need, nor to recognise its rising.

These questions about our lives, our source and ultimate end are spiritual in nature, coming from the noetic dimension of ourselves. Without purpose, without an ultimate context within which to live our lives, the daily bits and pieces of life seem unimportant and unrelated to each other. Meaning, noetic values and purpose tether us to points on the map, by which to navigate our living and our dying.

Constellations To Live By

Meaning points on the map of our lives act like stars to the sailor in the night sky. When we recognise only the physical and mental side of ourselves, we have our vessel that carries us. But when we add points of meaning in our life, we add the points of navigation we left and where we are headed, the sky above us and the sea below. It gives us coordinates to live by. We can say we are on our way to God, to being a better parent or a better version of ourselves; we can risk suffering for the love of others; we can strive to achieve but have no need of public glory because everything we do quietly rewards us. Meaning places our lives in the larger map of things. We know where we came from, and where we are headed. It give us our why and our how of living. And most importantly of all, meaning animates us towards spiritual growth in every domain of our lives.

12

Holistic HR

Spirituality in the Workplace

'... What I do is me: for that I came...'
— Gerard Manley Hopkins

Over the course of the past decade, we have seen a major shift in how people work. There are more people in the workforce than ever before, with an increasing number holding more than one part-time role, often without a set workplace, perhaps dividing themselves between working from home, the office and a local coffee shop. Even within large multinational corporations, the design of the workplace is changing, with employees often having no allocated desk but instead 'hot-desking' at whatever workspace is available in the moment.

There has been plenty said about the high expectations of the millennial generation, those born between the 1980s and the mid-90s, and the 'generation Z' who came after them – their demands for higher pay, more autonomy and a more meaningful workplace. But these are not just the demands of a few lucky generations – these are human needs, common to us all. As we continue to work harder for longer hours, workers no longer find it acceptable to 'leave our personal lives at the door'. The harder we work, the more we need work to work for us. It no longer suffices that our employment provides us with an income – we increasingly want our work to match our values and aspirations, to offer us a sense that what we do has a larger meaning and that it matters.

For decades, research in organisational psychology has provided us with ways to motivate ourselves and our teams, to create leaders and to manage stress. But until recently, we have been spiritually shy, unwilling or scared to speak about human spiritual needs in our work. Despite the spoken surge of popular opinion towards embracing diversity, business – and every other aspect of public life – has by and large chosen secularity over the diversity that true pluralism brings.

Until a very short time ago, we chose to leave our spiritual selves at home when we went to work. Yet it is almost impossible to tease apart what is spiritual from what is psychological; where the spiritual (either secular or religious) aspect of ourselves is negated, we are more likely to 'psychologise' spiritual themes. Hope, aspiration, morality, values, vocation, connectedness, discernment, authenticity, poignancy, compassion, love, purpose, meaning, and our place in the world – amongst other subjects – are spiritual matters common to all faiths and none, which are often sanitised into psychological language because we are too afraid to speak about what the vast majority of the world's population believe in – a spiritual dimension to life, be that atheistic, agnostic or religious.

Most companies certainly do their best to look after the mental and physical wellbeing and needs of their people. Many of the large multinationals offer their workforce subsidised canteens, on-site supermarkets, dry-cleaners and ping-pong tables, which all help to make working life a little easier and more enjoyable. No doubt these perks are welcome, but they give only the short-lived benefits of hedonic happiness. They are like the proverbial carrot on a string, an external motivator that can only keep people engaged for as long as they haven't discovered the fire-in-the-belly motivation of something that is personally meaningful and spiritually fulfilling. Despite the growing trend of 'mental health week' and lunchtime walking groups, in Europe we have yet to see a recognition of our spiritual dimension in the average workplace. Where are our spiritual health weeks? Where are our lunchtime philosophy clinics? When will we assess a candidate's spiritual intelligence? When will we learn that many of our career goals, much of our stress and mental health difficulties, as well as our need for personal growth, all come from a deep inner voice which cannot be silenced?

The Inevitable 'I' in Team

It is part of being human to crave meaning in our lives. As Viktor Frankl showed, even in the most inhumane conditions, our need for meaning continues and can provide us with the motivation to keep going in the most horrific conditions. Recent research has shown that meaningfulness is more important to employees than any other aspect of work, including pay, opportunities for promotion, and work conditions. Meaningfulness at work improves a person's job performance, engagement, motivation, personal fulfilment, sense of empowerment and job satisfaction. It decreases absenteeism and smooths the transition into retirement.

For some, meaning is found in developing the self, growing towards our potential. These people need to feel that they are active agents in their future, and that their work is in keeping with their sense of who they are and why they are in the world. They want to have their view of themselves and their strengths confirmed by their co-workers, and to enjoy a sense of autonomy over the tasks they carry out. They want to enjoy a sense of personal purpose.

In reality, however, many people are in low-paid jobs, often with little autonomy or sense of control. Meaning can feel a million miles away. But when we remember Frankl's idea of meaning being available to us not only in what we do, but also through our attitudes, we can use our seven pillars to change our experience of work by choosing the attitude we bring to it. Using each daily pillar imbues our life with meaning. It is a process of self-betterment for our own rewards, or in service to God or our higher power, or both.

Discovering our power to change

Carol is a 27-year-old sales assistant who was struggling with feelings of underachievement and a lack of motivation when we met. She felt that her career ambitions were stunted where she worked and she struggled to find meaning in a job that she believed had little prospects. Changing her attitude to work made her job enjoyable again. She explains how she began to recognise the power she had to change things and the impact those changes had on those around her.

> I work as a sales assistant in a high-end lingerie shop. I am surrounded by beautiful things that I can't afford to buy for myself as I have a young baby. I had hoped to work in a bigger store, where I could work my way up the career ladder into management; so I felt I was underachieving in this shop, was bored, and was really just biding my time to find something else.

When I started to look for more meaning in my work, the first thing I thought of was that the things I sold made women feel good about themselves. That helped me a bit, but it didn't really help me feel better about myself. When I started to choose what attitude (pillar) I was going to bring to work every day, I really began to notice a difference. Even when chatting to the other girls when things were quiet, my conversation was kinder and I felt good about myself. On days when I was practising patience I never gave up trying to find something that the customer loved – no matter how many times I had to go back to the shop floor. People really appreciated that and commented on how helpful I was. I got better at speaking with customers and I especially liked finding something nice for people who felt self-conscious about their shape. I kind of began to feel like their therapist! I used humour even if it wasn't the pillar for the day and that helped customers feel relaxed. I realised I had more power than I thought; I understood that women who are changing in and out of lingerie feel vulnerable, and that I could help them to feel good about themselves.

On one of my stillness days, I asked if we could change the music in the shop to restful music like you would hear in a beautician's, and now that's one of the CDs we play regularly. I really feel that I have come on a lot and I find it much easier to go into work every morning. I understand that I can set off a behaviour contagion-effect by changing how I deal with people. I also like to think of my pillars as my prayers because I usually forget to pray at night, or else I fall asleep in the middle of saying them.

What each of us considers meaningful is deeply personal and varies from person to person. It is usually found when what we do resonates with a broader context beyond ourselves. Meaning transcends the tyranny of individualism that has become the fashion of our times, and reinstates us in our role as part of a larger whole.

When researchers from the world-famous MIT asked people about the circumstances in which they found their work to be meaningful, they discovered that people tend to describe their work as meaningful when they could reflect on its wider contribution to society in ways that were personally relevant. The research also found meaning to be a temporary feeling, rather than a continuous state. But perhaps our transient experience of meaning at work is because we have not yet learned to find meaning in the mundane, and consider only the 'big lights' to be significant.

Meaning doesn't necessarily cause feelings of happiness. 'Poignancy' might be a more apt description of the feeling that meaning gives us – when our lives and our work resonate with our values. Meaning cannot be given by others – but it can be destroyed by poor management practises. Separating a person from their values, giving them pointless or tedious work, or work which does not make a contribution to the larger context; and putting workers in physical or emotional danger, or separating people from their supportive relationships, are some of the ways in which managers can destroy personal meaning for workers.

Several studies have shown the links between highly demanding work with little perceived reward, and an increased risk of cardiovascular disease. It seems that meaning, fulfilment, and our need for a sense of place in the world are wired in to our biology – a sort of psycho-spiritual immune system against disease.

One of psychology's most famous theories about what motivates us is known as the 'hierarchy of needs', proposed by American psychologist Abraham Maslow. Maslow suggested that each of us is motivated by different levels of needs, which he described as being like a pyramid, which we worked up through to higher and higher levels of needs.

According to Maslow's theory, as we meet the needs of one level, we progress to the next. At the lowest level of the hierarchy are our physiological needs, such as the need for food, water, rest and warmth. It is hard to focus on other things when we are hungry and cold. The next level is our safety needs, such as security and personal safety. Next are our belonging needs, including intimate relationships and friendships. Above these are our need for esteem, including prestige and feelings of accomplishment. At top of the pyramid Maslow placed our need for what he called 'self-actualisation'. Self-actualisation includes our need for creative activities and the opportunity to achieve our full potential.

In later years Maslow withdrew his idea that we cannot be interested in higher things, such as self-actualisation and self-esteem, until we have fulfilled the lower levels. In correspondence with Viktor Frankl, Maslow admitted that his theory didn't allow for the acts of compassion and self-transcendence which Frankl saw in people who were being starved to death.

Research in psychology also demonstrates that people in catastrophes will sometimes show immense courage and generosity towards others, rather than simply looking after themselves. But Maslow was not entirely wrong with his hierarchy of needs theory. When our capacities are stretched to the maximum in simply trying to survive, to feed our children or to pay the mortgage, philosophical conversations on the highest meanings of life can feel like luxuries we can't afford.

Maslow placed our physical and safety needs at the widest, lowest level of his hierarchy because these needs apply to all of us, whereas, according to his theory, a much smaller number of people manage to meet all their lower needs and achieve self-actualisation. But in terms of our spiritual lens, the lower levels are like the narrow-focused beam of a spotlight, which allows little else to be seen other than the need to put food on the table and a roof over our heads.

These lowest level survival needs are fear-driven. In the work environment, these most basic needs might result in taking any job, just so that we can pay the bills or feel that we work in a physically safe space. As we move up the hierarchy, the tightness of fearful thinking gives way to a more expansive lens. Free from immediate survival needs, we are able to think about what we aspire to, why we are here, and other more philosophical conversations. It is like widening the beam of the spotlight to take in other things – the figure and ground of gestalt again. When we are freed from the lacking of the lower levels and what Maslow called our deficiency needs, we are able to consider how we can stretch ourselves to fulfil our potential, which Maslow called our growth, or being, needs.

Maslow noticed two different types or levels of people who could be called self-actualisers. The first type he called 'non-transcenders'. These are people who are indeed achieving their full potential, but with a pragmatic, concrete, here-and-now approach. They fulfil their unique, personal potential in a practical way, doing good and using life for good purposes.

The second type of self-actualised people Maslow called 'transcenders'. These were perhaps more likely to have an appreciation of Being itself, and to have had peak (euphoric) and plateau (serene, contemplative) experiences. According to Maslow, transcenders are able to see the sacred in the mundane, and to see the unity of all things. They can also see things relative to eternity, and yet at the same time are able to make practical judgements when needed. Transcenders are motivated by what Maslow called 'metamotivations', such as beauty, truth and goodness, rather than the needs of the ego, and tend to be viewed by others with a sense of awe, love or saintliness.

On the other hand, while transcenders can be happier than others, Maslow considered these individuals to be prone to a sort of cosmic sadness, on account of the cruelty and pain that they see in the world which stand in stark contrast to the wide-ranging potentials and expansive ideals they can so easily imagine. Increasing knowledge draws transcenders closer to a corresponding increased sense of mystery and awe at the world; whereas for the non-transcending self-actualiser – as for those lower on the hierarchy – knowledge tends to give a sense of being on top of everything, thus weakening awe.

In order to self-actualise, the individual needs to leave behind self-consciousness and self-centredness, yet still retain a sense of themselves, so that they can become aware of the difference between their own judgement and the internalised voices of a parent, society, or other various external judges and juries.

Self-actualised people tend to live a life that is more authentic to their true selves. They nurture their personal strengths. These attributes don't suddenly appear, but accumulate over time, through the decisions that they make and the actions they choose to take.

In Maslow's hierarchy, people can get stuck at any level. They can meet their esteem needs but not progress into self-actualisation. Where the person is unaware of their noetic needs, the unconscious questions about the meaning of life and their existence can often become a problem, causing mental ill-health, depression, and what Maslow called 'meta-pathologies'. These are spiritual or existential crises of meaninglessness and valuelessness, caused by our unmet needs of the human spirit. It is quite possible that to some extent at least, these noetic issues may be a root cause of the high rates of suicide in our society.

There is no end point or finished product in Maslow's view of development. The self-actualised non-transcending individual may or may not progress to be a self-actualised transcender, and the transcenders never stop developing their value-driven life. Both types can have peak and plateau experiences, but for the transcender, these peak experiences become the focus of their life. But according to Maslow, all self-actualised people – having met their lower, more basic needs of food, safety, esteem, etc – have a focus that is outside of themselves; a cause greater than themselves, to which they feel a certain calling or vocation. Their motivations then become 'meta-motivations', such as world peace and justice, a love of the world but also a desire to improve it, an enjoyment of doing good and trying to stop cruelty, a love of practical tasks that work towards these goals, a sense of duty, and a respect for mystery.

Without the intrusion of fears and ego, transcenders can see reality as true, beautiful, integrated, alive, good, perfect, etc, as opposed to these being qualities the world should have. For Maslow, transcendent self-actualisation is simply being authentic to our biology – it is a way of being deeply immersed in nature that we are a part of. It is innately good for us and feels right when we experience transcendent self-actualisation. When we see self-actualising transcendence in this way, we don't need to use distancing words such as 'highest' or 'supernatural' to describe what these people achieve; they are actually going more deeply into their true nature, rather than escaping it in some way.

Maslow was an atheist, but he saw the spiritual life as part of our human essence, part of our real self. The qualities he described of the self-actualised transcender are every bit as real as any other topic studied by science; and they are available to all of us through effort, whether we are religious or not.

Contrary to the popular belief that the transcender

type of personality is rare, Maslow believed that self-actualised transcenders are found in all walks of life – from trade and services to business, teaching and politics, as much as in the religious, creative or artistic set, where we might be more inclined to look for them. Unfortunately, we mentally separate these worlds, so that the more enlightened temperament of the transcender is not expected, or even welcome, in the worlds of business and politics, where they may feel unable to speak about how they see the world.

The Seven Pillars at Work: Noetic Management Practises

Any business organisation is a semi-permeable living entity, much like a human cell. A company can never exist in isolation, but depends upon its workforce, suppliers and customers – the local and global environment – for its survival. A company must be conscious of the larger context which surrounds it if it wants to be successful. Self-transcendence is as much a part of the healthy workplace as it is a part of the fulfilled human being. The permeability of the workplace gives its employees the opportunity to meet their spiritual needs, and to turn their work life into the main method by which they make a meaningful impact in the world.

At work, we may already have created, or else have the ability to create, several sources of meaning. We might practise being kind to someone who annoys us as a way to improve ourselves, or in keeping with religious beliefs. We might take on a client or customer who cannot pay their way, because it allows us to send kindness out into the world. When looking for work, we may have applied to a shortlist of companies that we knew had environmental policies or other values in keeping with our own. Meaning is for us to make in everything we do – cc'ing someone in an email list to make them feel included; nodding and smiling at a colleague who is struggling through a presentation; asking how someone is and then waiting for them to answer; being patient with an overly chatty patient; staying longer at work to help a co-worker; experiencing awe at the uniqueness of every individual; standing up for someone who is being talked over; taking overtime hours because it pays for our children's field trip; reducing the use of environmentally harmful cleaning chemicals, or introducing recycled paper into a company – these are all ways in which we can build meaning into our work.

What we already do is not growth, it is stagnation. It can be easy to show patience to a customer who needs help, or share humour with someone we like. But growth means challenging ourselves to do more, to do better than the things that we already do. Making the effort to share a joke with someone who we don't normally get on with, or struggling to forgive someone we don't want to forgive, is truly developing the Seven-Day Soul. It means pushing the envelope to reach for more than the low-hanging fruit, adding values instead of value, and striving for excellence, even when there is no end point where we can say we have achieved our goals.

Every business, from the sole trader to the multinational conglomerate, can be seen as existing somewhere on Maslow's hierarchy. Many business owners have a great desire to do good work and to be of service – after they have made enough money to start giving it away. But this idea – that tending to our noetic needs and acts of self-transcendence should be delayed until we are successful – is outdated. It is not simply about working for free or making donations. A 'transcender' culture in work should not rely on 'Jane in Accounts' or 'Brian in Marketing' being 'really into environmental issues' or 'raising money for a sponsored cycle'.

While these types of projects raise a large portion of funds for charities and show the power that one individual can have, noetic management means that the noetic dimension of the business and of the individual is built in to how we design our corporate structure; in other words, the noetic is incorporated into our business plan. Mission statements are no longer simply words on a wall, but act instead as graphs which we can use as yardsticks to measure our growth.

The noetic business makes corporate and social responsibility a foundation of its business model, alongside, but not instead of, profit. It recognises its people as operating at different levels of needs, but all having the potential for transcendence within them. The transcendent leader doesn't simply work on themselves, but works to lift others up to their fullest potential. This is itself an act of generosity, going against our natural fearful tendency to grab the limelight for ourselves. Instead, she or he raises the spiritual intelligence of everyone.

Maslow recommended that we should use 'eupsychian' management techniques (*eu*-meaning good in Greek, and the *psyche* meaning mind *and* heart), whereby an organisation gives full recognition to the individual's higher needs for self-actualisation. Maslow said that we can tell which stage of the hierarchy a person is living at by what makes them laugh. If we laugh at a joke which not only has a punchline but also a punchbag – a victim of the joke – then we have not reached self-actualisation. Laughing at someone getting hurt or ridiculed is a sign of someone who has not left behind the need for power, prestige and status. Higher-level jokes have no need of hostility, conquest or a victim.

Similarly, a manager can gauge the level of health at which their company is functioning by the complaints they receive from employees. Higher needs would revolve around issues such as dignity, autonomy, honesty, injustice, and standing up for someone else, rather than the sandwich selection available in the canteen. Human beings will always complain, but there is a difference between 'grumbles' and the higher, more self-transcendent 'meta-grumbles'.

Some businesses can connect their business model more easily to a transcendent aim than others. In recent years there has been an increase in social enterprises whose very existence is based on making the world a better place – such as by increasing the use of solar power, microfinancing small businesses in third-world countries, or creating ethical investment options for investors. Some jobs from the outside seem naturally more meaningful than others – policing, healthcare and the emergency services are all easily connected to self-transcendence. But there is no business that cannot incorporate the seven pillars, making the pillars their watermark on every business day.

When engaged in any task – whether designing a new product, making a team decision, or organising a work roster – the whole company should adopt the daily pillar to uphold and inform everything that is done that day. A company might choose to start all meetings with a minute of silence, so that everyone can have the chance to still themselves, and become aware of the hurriedness that often alters how we behave in a meeting. The policy might extend to inviting staff or visitors in the car park to take a reflective minute, by placing notices requesting that people pause before getting out of their cars; or on a gratitude day, signs that suggest taking a moment to think about things to be grateful for before getting out of the car.

The pillar of the day could be displayed at reception as a reminder to everyone who passes that this is what the whole company will focus on for the day. The hold button could let callers know that this is a company working on itself for the benefit of all. Certain days of the week could have themes, like 'forgiveness Friday'. Canteen staff might choose to ice the pillar of the day on cakes, or even have some fun giving the daily offerings names such as 'patience pie' or 'funny flapjacks'. Spirituality and meaning are often thought of as serious, heady topics, but our ability to find humour in things, to see things differently, is part of what makes us human. It is a crucial skill in helping to shift us out of the fearful thinking of a stressed mind, into a more noetic way of doing business, and of moving each and every employee nearer to their potential.

The more a person can consider the end user of their work, the more likely it is that they'll be able to instil some of the more tedious work tasks with meaning. Tasks that seem tedious can be made meaningful when we look at them as a means to serve or satisfy the end user or customer, or a means to pay for things for those we love; or as an exercise in patience, compassion or service. It is how we appraise the potential significance of a task that creates the meaning.

A good example of this is the yearly practise by Medtech, a publicly listed, multibillion dollar US medical devices company. Medtech's annual meetings are attended by over 1,600 people, and are viewed by thousands of other employees over CCTV links. At these meetings, a small group of patients whose lives have been saved or helped by Medtech products are invited to speak about how the Medtech team's work has benefitted them. Also at the meetings, the Medtech CEO provides examples of how the work of each individual in the company contributed to those patient benefits.

This is a large-scale example of cultivating meaning at work. But meaning doesn't require sweeping or costly gestures. A carer for someone with dementia might choose to ask detailed questions of the family about the dementia sufferer's preferences, before their condition made it difficult to answer these questions themselves. The carer could find out, for example, what sort of music their client used to listen to, or whether or not they liked to wear nail varnish; and in this way make their attention towards every person in their care individual and personal.

In the office, sending an email to someone's inbox is like having a key to someone's front door and sitting in their kitchen waiting for them to come home. How much do you respect other people's virtual space – and their mental health? Have you ever reconsidered sending an unnecessary email, thereby playing your part in deconstructing our always-available, stressful lives? Perhaps this can be one of your pillar of generosity acts for a day.

In a study looking at the impact of meaning and lack of meaning at work, three US researchers set up artificial, repetitive task experiments, which they designed to have varying, but very low, degrees of meaning. Their first experiment looked at whether the supply of workers for a tedious and repetitive task could be altered by changing the degree of meaning within the task. Ninety-four students were divided into three groups. In each group, participants were given a sheet of paper with a seemingly random sequence of letters on it, and told that they would be paid fifty-five cents for finding ten instances of two consecutive letters S. When they had completed the first page, they were asked whether they would be willing to complete a second page for fifty cents. With each subsequent page that they agreed to complete, they were offered payment that decreased by five cents each time.

Subjects in the first group were asked to put their names on each sheet before beginning the task (which increases our sense of ownership of a piece of work). Before starting, the instructions explained that after they had completed the sheet, they would hand the sheet over to the experimenter, who would examine it and file it away in a folder. In the second group, the subjects were not instructed to write their names on the sheet, and were told that on completion, the experimenter would place their sheet on a high stack of papers. The third group were similarly not instructed to put their names on a page, and were also told that when they turned in their sheet, the experimenter would shred the sheet without looking at it.

All subjects completed the task individually. Taking the three situations together, we would expect that the first group might give up first, as their work was more personally demanding (because their name was on the sheet). But the results of the study showed the opposite. Almost half of the subjects in this first group continued to work until the wage dropped all the way to zero, and completed more sheets than either of the other two groups. The other two groups worked to a similar level of pay as each other, but stopped at a pay level of almost twice that of the first group. For the first group, it seems that putting their names to their work instantly made it more meaningful, and they were therefore willing to work for much less payment. The blatant, almost abusive act of shredding the work of the third group showed very little difference to placing the second group's work on a stack of paper; for all of these participants, the effects on motivation were disastrous.

In a second experiment by the same researchers, study

participants were required to assemble Bionicle Lego toys. The toys, when assembled by the participants, were either placed in front of them on the table so that they could see their work accumulating, or were immediately disassembled and the pieces placed in a box, so that the participant was always reassembling toys that had been disassembled by the experimenter. In both situations, participants were offered payment that decreased with each subsequent toy assembled.

The results showed that even when the task was the same, and the pay decreased by the same amount for each group, the individuals working in the more meaningful situation – where they could see their work accumulating – built significantly more toys, and continued to work for significantly less money, than participants in the other group. In the meaningful group, the average worker stopped when they were paid $1.01 per item, while the meaningless group stopped working at $1.40 on average. The researchers concluded that the individuals in the meaningless work group became sensitive to the trade-off between time and money more quickly. The money simply wasn't worth the effort.

Work is more than a time for money exchange. This study showed that altering other factors, such as making the work slightly more meaningful and more obviously productive, even when it is equally repetitive, increases our willingness to keep going. Visible outcomes and considering the end user is a great way to help ourselves to find meaning in the mundane aspects of our work.

· · · · · · · · · · · · · ·On Reflection· · · · · · · · · · · · · ·

Visible Outcomes

If you were to sign your name on every piece of plastic that you use – every water bottle, butter tub, shampoo bottle, coffee lid, bin bag, dog poop bag, loose fruit bag, and on and on – and collected them together in a pile, would it change how much plastic you use?

None of us want to harm the planet, and many of us will have cut back on some plastic use. But we cannot sit back and congratulate ourselves on our small victories. There is far more left to do.

Finding spiritual purpose and the meaning of our lives is a process that never ends. Purpose and meaning need to be coaxed out of the mundanity of our everyday lives. Spiritual growth is not so much in the momentous, luminous epiphanies where we feel passion and clarity – these moments are the rest and recharge area for the remainder of life. Real spiritual growth is more often in suffering, in mundane or repetitive work, that forces us out of our own comforts and into the service of the world around us.

The Spirituality Movement

In the US, many organisations actively welcome religious membership and practise, and research in the area is flourishing. In these workplaces, religious and/

or spiritual beliefs are ingrained in the essence of their business model and are the foundation stones of their purpose, such as making the world a more equitable place. This purpose directs every part of their business day: prayer breakfasts, higher power lunches and interfaith discussion groups are part and parcel of the working day. Training days are dedicated to spiritual development, which also becomes a key component of leadership training and recruitment programmes. A 2004 research study with mid- and senior level executives in a US federal government agency showed that executives there linked spirituality to success, which they described using words like 'wholeness', being 'connected' and 'balance'.

Spiritually oriented companies vary in the degree to which they overtly address religion, and some prefer to speak about 'spirituality' over specific religious teachings. Others are overtly Catholic, Quaker, Hindu, etc. But there is no doubt that the integration of spirituality into business life is gaining in popularity. The longer we spend at work, the more work must offer us opportunities for fulfilment, wellbeing and contribution to the world. While we can be proud of the arrival of mindfulness meditation into the mainstream, in most instances it is merely a brain-training, stress-reduction exercise, with little acknowledgement of its deeply spiritual grounding. Moving spirituality centre stage in the world of work requires that we don't fluff our words, or use meditation as a safe middle ground that sounds vaguely spiritual but doesn't demand that we go any further. Mainstreaming spirituality into our workplaces demands a much deeper sea change in how we view our humanness, and the introduction of the vocabulary necessary to do so. Our noetic life is a fundamental human dimension, not some marshmallow sweet notion or 'soft skill' sprinkled on top of our more serious physical and mental health. We have noetic needs. The feelings of emptiness and pointlessness that can lead to suicide in people who seem to 'have it all' are symbols of unmet noetic needs that lead to an existential void even when all of our financial, mental and physical needs have been met and surpassed.

Management theorists have predicted a shift in the way we work, from transactional leadership (a straightforward trade of work for payment) to transformational leadership, and from an economically focused business model, where simply making money was enough, to a balancing of profits with quality of life, spirituality and social responsibility. This new approach has been called 'The Spirituality Movement' and described as the 'most significant trend in management since the fifties'.

Whether secular or religious, spirituality is a growing trend in business that is redefining our image of what progress is. It can no longer be defined in narrow terms of economic profits. Progress has gained a girth that expands it outwards to include profit but which also demands other deliverables: meaning, authenticity, values, compassion, community, inner life, and the opportunity to contribute to something larger than oneself. As such, our view of progress is set to become increasingly more self-transcendent. This noetic workplace of the future will offer poignant work, and although it may also introduce new challenges, it will also reap the benefits of growth, efficiency, and return on investment that research has shown to be typical of spiritual workplaces. Spirituality cannot be introduced as some cynical ploy to increase productivity – any such attempts have been shown in research to have the opposite effect on motivation – we know when we are being conned. But the company that changes its way of doing business from its core is likely to enjoy the animating energy of a workforce newly (re)orientated to meta-values, be they terrestrial or metaphysical. Where there are people, there is spirit – human spirit that needs and wants to be unfolded out to what it can be in its fullness.

On Reflection

Workplace Ministry

'Workplace ministry' is a phrase normally used to describe the role of an in-house pastor or religious teacher, employed by a company to look after the spiritual needs of a workforce. But in what way can you see your working day as your personal spiritual workplace ministry? Whether we have religious beliefs or are SBNR, we all have a role to play in moving the modern workplace towards being a more holistic and loving force in the service of something more than itself. The seven pillars of generosity, gratitude, forgiveness, patience, awe, humour and stillness are our daily to-do list.

13
Spirituality in Education
The Playground of the Soul

It seems ironic that our emphasis on academic skills and the intellect has brought us to the point of our own undoing. Artificial intelligence (AI) is both the pinnacle of human intellectual achievement, and also possibly the end of the era of humankind as creator.

Over the course of time, the advent of AI will also show us that it is not the *doing* of a task that makes us human. If computers are destined to take over the bulk of human work, then our education system must provide an infrastructure that supports our evolution in another direction. When intelligence is computed, where else can we evolve?

If we were to search online for images of progress, we would quickly see that our society's mental model of progress is always upwards. Images of graphs, arrows and staircases lead us to believe that progress means doing more of what we are already doing. But if we are serious about ecological concerns and the betterment of society, then we may need to look at expanding the breadth, as well as the height, of our image of progress.

If evolution is really moving towards a more holistic consciousness of connectedness – and, arguably, if we are to survive as a species – then the direction of our education system must change to nurture not only human rights, but also human responsibilities. We need to raise the coming generations to see that with the rights that most of us enjoy in Western society come responsibilities to serve those behind us, who still struggle for their most fundamental rights.

There will be times when current teachings on wellness and self-care will collide with teachings on love, as service to others surpasses development of the self in social value. Development of the self will come to be understood as a side-effect of service to the other. Moral development will need to be the cornerstone of education. Traits such as wisdom, justice, discernment, empathy, compassion and service will need to come to the fore. But this will not happen until popular thought is moved; and it is how we educate our young people today that will accelerate or delay this expansion of the girth of progress.

It is not so much that we need to educate our young people spiritually; it is that we need to stop de-educating their innate spirituality out of them. Every parent who has ever brought a young child for a walk is familiar with the open fascination that children have for the world. Walks can seem painfully slow, as the parent with the goal of a walk around the park is forced to stop over and over again while their little one leaves no stone unturned in their investigations.

We tend to presume that children cannot be spiritual until they can understand religious language. But this really just reflects our own generation's belief that spirituality is about a set of beliefs – things to be known. Children might certainly struggle with mystical concepts described in language as intellectual ideas, but they can be innately, non-linguistically spiritual. They just don't need to give it a name. In fact, this is a more true spirituality – spirituality as another way of experiencing, another way of seeing, everyday life. This lens on the world weakens as children progress through our education system, internalising society's misunderstanding of scientific thought as being contrary to spirituality.

In order to better educate our children, and thereby protect and foster their innate spirituality, we first need to re-educate ourselves. If we hope to raise future generations to be more self-aware, and more compassionate to others and the environment, then we need to make conscious choices about our education system, just as we do about our personal lives. If we don't tell young people that they have spiritual needs, then how can they explain their feelings of loss, emptiness or meaninglessness? We need to adjust their lens on the world to a more unitive setting, one which focuses on the development of self-knowledge in relationship to others and to the world. If spirituality is as innate in young children as it appears to be – and given that we know it to be a source of wellbeing for the individual and for society – then it is not just our opportunity, but our duty, to develop spirituality in children.

Developing Our Spiritual Intelligence in the Seven-Day Soul

Since the early 1980s, psychologists have accepted the idea of there being more than one type of intelligence. We can have linguistic, logical-mathematical, musical, spatial, intrapersonal, and other types of intelligence. In 1999, Robert Emmons described a new type, which he called 'spiritual intelligence'. Since then, many other writers have tried to capture and measure this. All of these writers have looked upon it as a blending type of intelligence, one which integrates our rational and emotional types of intelligence so that it forms the link between mind, body, heart and soul.

Robert Emmons spoke of five characteristics of spiritual intelligence:

1. **The capacity to transcend the physical and material**

In the Seven-Day Soul, we live in awareness of the vertical and horizontal life planes, so that everything we do in our everyday life (the horizontal plane) is informed by an awareness of a higher dimension (the vertical plane). A person's higher dimension may be considered divine, or just a more evolved version of what we can be.

2. **The ability to experience heightened states of consciousness**
Our meditation and prayer practises actively invite higher states of consciousness, which we might at first only get fleeting moments of, but which, with practise, become more visible in the horizontal life plane. We begin to understand that higher states of consciousness can act as our lenses in the most mundane situations, rather than being exceptional rare moments, or for a select few people only.

3. **The ability to sanctify everyday experiences**
Every moment of the day becomes an opportunity to practise our seven pillars. Every conversation, every task, becomes a service to something more than ourselves, and we learn to see the world with awe-filled eyes.

4. **The ability to utilise spiritual resources to solve problems**

   Living in respect of more than one dimension of reality can slow down our reactivity, helping us to make wiser, more considered judgements which take both life planes into consideration.

5. **The capacity to be virtuous**

   Being virtuous isn't some instantly identifiable state that a person suddenly drops into. It is a path we build, brick by brick, as we walk through life. Every moment patiently gives us another chance to be a better version of ourselves. Every fork in the path presents us with a decision to be made about how we will act. Aiming at virtue is a noble intention, but if we don't have a path, it will remain a pipe dream. The seven pillars of generosity, gratitude, forgiveness, patience, awe, humour and stillness are the bricks which build our path.

If we want to increase the spiritual intelligence of future generations (and ourselves), there are three aspects that we need to develop:

1. **Inner life**

   Our inner life is the study of our being. In order to be compassionate when our patience

is really being tested, we need to have
developed a degree of self-awareness, control,
and inner peace. What are the lenses we have
developed or inherited over our lifetime?
What are our biases? Is it possible for us to
differentiate between fact and opinion? We
often describe ourselves as being 'moved' by
something. If we pay enough attention, we
can see that emotions come with physical
sensations, which we can learn to use as
signposts to our inner life. As we cultivate
self-awareness, we gain the courage to act
autonomously to popular opinion.

2. **Outer life**
Spirituality is about the how of our living.
It concerns how we use our seven pillars to
inform our interactions with others, so that
we are responsible and conscious of the social
contagion which we set in motion by what
we do, think and say. Our outer life concerns
our *doing* in the world, and our ability to
experience being part of the physical world we
live in, including our ability to sense harmony
and awe. Our outer lives offer us the chance
to live our days with our values in mind, and
to imbue even the suffering in our lives with a
sense of meaning.

3. **The transcendent**

This aspect of our spiritual life may be our relationship to the divine, or to another overarching reality, such as love or oneness. It includes beliefs in being from, or part of, an ultimate reality; understandings about the purpose of our existence; and the meaning that naturally emanates from these convictions. For some, the transcendent might be more about questions than answers – questions about why we are here. Whether or not we have religious beliefs, we learn to cultivate the transcendent – a whole-seeing lens on all of existence – so that even the most humdrum activity is seen in relation to a larger context.

'The necessary Utopia'

In 1996, the International Commission on Education for the Twenty-first Century published a report for UNESCO, entitled *Learning: The Treasure Within*. The report called for a renewed emphasis on the 'moral and cultural dimensions of education, enabling each person to grasp the individuality of other people and to understand the world's erratic progression towards a certain unity'. But, said the report, 'this process must begin with self–understanding through an inner voyage whose milestones are knowledge, meditation and the practise of self-criticism'.

The report highlighted self-knowledge as an important new subject to be prioritised in education, so that we can learn to balance the tensions between competition and equality; tradition and modernity; concern for the universal and protecting the need for belonging of every individual. Self-knowledge teaches us to see what we ourselves bring to a situation, and to question ourselves before we question others. But it is also, according to the report, about giving a voice to our need for ideals and moral values, which are so often unexpressed. In this, the commission was calling for the expansion of our spiritual vocabulary, to help us manage the tension which we all live with, between the material and the spiritual dimensions of our lives.

It is thus education's noble task to encourage each and every one, acting in accordance with their own traditions and convictions and paying full respect to pluralism, to lift their minds and spirits to the plane of the universal and, in some measure, to transcend themselves. It is no exaggeration on the Commission's part to say that the survival of humanity depends on it.

The commission recommended that education be based on four pillars: learning to know, learning to do, learning to be, and lear... particular emphasis on our need t... We need to be able to deal with inevi... an intelligent and peaceful way, and to deve... of interdependence and understanding of others – history, their traditions and their spiritual values. This the commission called a 'necessary Utopia', which we need in order to escape the dangerous cycle of cynicism and resignation.

Cynicism is the easiest path for any of us, and as such it is the laziest mode of thinking. Cynicism demands nothing of us, but simply feeds on our fear that we might fail in our aspirations. It is worse than resignation because it pretends to be thoughtful judgement. Judgement is a conscious, self-aware process, where we patiently and methodically consider a matter, its pros and cons, and the lens which we bring to it. Cynicism, on the other hand, is hiding behind the safety of doubt, in the anonymity of the numbered masses. It is tempting for any of us to be cynical because we can simply stay as we are, risking nothing.

To combat cynicism, we need, just as the commission said, to teach ourselves to tune in again to our inner voice, that part of us connected to something common to us all, which includes but transcends the intellect of the head. We need to develop in ourselves the courage to listen to the pull of the heart towards the good.

...ot happen
Each of us
...ation in self-
...catch ourselves
...s, and notice the
...k at ourselves. Just
...r national education
...ts to the plane of the
..., require a re-education
in... ...ot what to think). As our
econom... ...y global, we need to develop
future genera... ...rientate themselves to higher
values which are... universal, being common to all
humanity. Mahatma Gandhi once defined education as
the 'all round drawing out of the best in the child and
man – body, mind and spirit'. The word 'educate' comes
from the Latin word *educare*, which means to nurture
or bring out. We need to balance collation of knowledge
with methods which nurture rather than destroy the
higher callings of every individual. We cannot do this if
we do not tell a child these callings exist.

**When we talk about a total human being, we
mean not only a human being with inward
understanding, with a capacity to explore, to
examine his or her inward state and the capacity of
going beyond it, but also someone who is good in
what he does outwardly. The two must go together.**

That is the real issue in education: to see that when the child leaves the school, he is well established in goodness, both outwardly and inwardly.
— **J. Krishnamurti, Indian philosopher, (1895–1986),** *on education*

The development of spiritual intelligence does not mean that we should cast away the education of our students in skills and competencies that are already part of the curriculum, but only that we need to simultaneously develop methods by which students can learn about their spiritual needs. Our education system can no longer throw a few vague notions of spirituality towards our children, but must instead fully integrate this aspect of intelligence into the curriculum, as a high-value component which acts as a magnetic north in the educational lifetime of the child. If we are serious in our concerns for the direction in which our society is heading, and the rising rates of depression, anxiety and suicide, and ongoing wars, then we need to look again at what spiritual intelligence can offer us — at any stage of life.

· · · · · · · · · · · · · · · On Reflection · · · · · · · · · · · · · · ·

Kindness Cops and the Sunshine Sheriff
For young children (but also adults)

This reflection can be adapted to be done as a morning

prayer, with a kiss goodbye at the school gates, or as a classroom exercise at the start of the day.

Let each of us turn on our kindness spotlights in search of people who need our kindness today. Sometimes we will need a strong beam to see people who need our kindness. Other times they will be easy to spot. Sometimes they will be the loud people, other times they will be quiet. Sometimes they will be young, and sometimes much older than us. Often these people will not ask for help, so we have to find them ourselves. They need our spotlight of kindness beamed on them. We will wear our kindness spotlight like a head torch on our foreheads, and it will come everywhere with us. [Loudly] We are the kindness cops. Let's get to work!

In the classroom, each child can take a turn at being the 'sunshine sheriff' for a day. The teacher might make a sheriff's badge which the delegated child is presented with at the start of the day. The sunshine sheriff is responsible for reminding everyone to keep checking their torches, to make sure they are still working throughout the day. At the start of break time and lunch times, the sunshine sheriff motivates the kindness cops to never forget there is work to be done. They have the power to change the world

14

Spirituality in Government

Governing for the Greater Good

'What a society honours will be cultivated.'

– Aristotle

It may seem counterintuitive to include government in matters of the soul, but as keeper of the national purse strings, the values and interests of a government certainly matter. A government may be the representative body of the majority, but it also has the opportunity to lead; to protect the quieter voices; and to hold open the space for minority opinions. When Nelson Mandela was freed from prison in South Africa in 1990, the weight of the majority was leaning heavily towards civil war, black people against white. But Mandela led his followers away from war, and despite some atrocities carried out by individuals, South Africa avoided what could have been deemed a 'just war' – an eye for an eye.

The role of good governance is not simply public representation, but also good leadership. This is an important difference. By its nature, a government must take a gestalt, holistic view of a nation, in a constant balancing and rebalancing act of interests. A government must position itself to uphold values, protecting against dangerous pendulum swings and reactive, volatile moods in public opinion. It must balance the sometimes competing demands of the needs of the moment with longer-term goals, which might demand restraint in the now. This is a difficult task considering that members of government must also keep an eye on their re-election. But members of government are in the unique position of having a public platform from which they can at least attempt to lead or influence public opinion, and to create movements in a nation's tides of thought.

In Roman times, in the first century AD, a slave stood in the chariot behind the triumphant general during a victory procession. The slave's role was to hold a golden crown over the general's head while whispering in his ear, 'Respice post te. Hominem te memento,' meaning, 'Look behind you. Remember you are human.' The practise was intended to act as a dose of humility for the triumphant general, to remind him that pride sometimes comes before a fall, and that despite his victory, he was still a fragile mortal.

When an economy is riding high, we may all, along

with our elected public representatives, need a similar whisper in our ear, to reorientate ourselves towards the ultimate values of love, compassion, and the evolution of human consciousness towards the common good.

We need leaders who are willing to use spiritual language, and to reference things of a spiritual nature. These are not 'soft' matters unconnected to our everyday living. When we ignore humanity's need to look beyond the immediate, or to ask questions about why we are here (the ability that differentiates us from all other species), an existential vacuum results – or what might otherwise be called an empty heart.

For Viktor Frankl, addiction, aggression and depression are society's symptoms of a life without meaning. Traditionally, religion provided people with answers to life's big questions and offered a path to follow. The challenge is to find a pluralism which includes secularists and theists with equal welcome, diluting neither, while respecting our common search for what is loving. Love is not a word that is often used in public life, and it will take courage for public representatives and every one of us to begin to introduce it into common usage. But when we appreciate that love is as fundamental a human need as gravity or air, we might begin to give love back its proper position as the ultimate advisor of every law and every decision we might make as a society.

Applied spirituality is the engagement of spiritual

teachings, without the dogma of specific religious traditions. This will take leadership and courage, but we could at the very least begin with verbal nods of recognition towards the spiritual domain by public representatives.

In 2007, speaking at a 'structured dialogue with churches, faith communities and non-confessional bodies', then Taoiseach Bertie Ahern said that Ireland was suffering from:

> ... *a form of aggressive secularism which would have the State and State institutions ignore the importance of the religious dimension. They argue that the State and public policy should become intolerant of religious belief and preference, and confine it, at best, to the purely private and personal, without rights or a role within the public domain. Such illiberal voices would diminish our democracy. They would deny a crucial dimension of the dignity of every person and their rights to live out their spiritual code within a framework of lawful practise, which is respectful of the dignity and rights of all citizens. It would be a betrayal of the best traditions of Irish republicanism to create such an environment.*

We should not confuse the separation of church and state with the renunciation of our noetic needs.

Is 'Happy' Out?

Happiness has become something of a buzzword. In 2012, the first *World Happiness Report* was published to coincide with a United Nations meeting. In 2016, the Organisation for Economic Cooperative and Development (OECD) committed to redefine our idea of growth, and to put people's wellbeing at the centre of government's efforts. Their 2018 report ranked 156 countries according to subjective studies on dimensions including GDP, life expectancy, generosity, social support, freedom and corruption. It also measured the happiness levels of immigrants in 117 of these countries.

Since 1971, the government of Bhutan has refused to measure gross domestic product (GDP) and instead measures gross national happiness (GNH) as its yardstick of progress. Measuring happiness is certainly a step in the direction of a more meaning-oriented economy. It correctly prioritises people over economic pursuit. We know that without some level of economic development, happiness becomes less likely, just as Maslow described. But above a certain point, increases in financial wealth cease to provide us with corresponding increases in happiness. Happiness is linked to economic growth to a certain point, beyond which the link grows weaker. In the 2017 *World Happiness Report*, China's strong GDP growth did not result in corresponding increases in subjective feelings of wellbeing among Chinese people.

> 'As indexed by GDP, wellbeing in China has multiplied over five-fold, but based on SWB (subjective wellbeing), is, on average, less than a quarter of a century ago.'
>
> – World Happiness Report 2017

Studies have shown that religious and spiritual beliefs do not necessarily bring us happiness – they offer us meaning, sense-making, support, rules to live by, aspirations to aim for, solace in suffering, and the prioritisation of love. We have already discussed the difference between happiness of the belly laugh variety and eudaimonia, the quieter, deeper contentment of spirit; and we know from psychological studies that it is not possible to be happy all the time, as our moods will naturally fluctuate.

So perhaps instead of positing happiness as the ultimate aspiration, we should design a values-driven society, which includes noetic values, where the dimensions of the human spirit that aspire to higher versions of ourselves are once again centre stage. This does not ignore the economic concerns of a nation, but ensures that they are operated in meaningful ways, in keeping with selected noetic aspirations.

> 'Not until the laws made by man are consistent with the laws made by a Higher Authority will we live in a just world.'
>
> – Dr Martin Luther King

State of Grace

E.F. Schumacher was an economist and philosopher who criticised the supposedly peaceful use of atomic energy as an example of the dictatorship of economics. For Schumacher, there was more to life than GDP. Schumacher was a natural philosopher – perhaps what Maslow might have called a 'transcender'. His deep fascination for the big existential questions of life and his human-centred economics made him something of a guru in his day. He was born in Germany, but moved to England to avoid living under the Nazi regime. These were the war years, and foreigners in England were viewed with suspicion. Schumacher, like many others, was interred in a British prisoner of war camp.

Despite the squalor and hardship, Schumacher, much like Viktor Frankl, found meaning in trying to give some order to the camps, writing in a letter to his wife that his efforts were 'based on kindness and persuasion . . . with so much misery about I am convinced it is the only method'. Being allowed to send letters home, Schumacher clearly did not experience first-hand the far greater destruction of humanity which Frankl experienced in Nazi Germany, but for both men, their imprisonment became a turning point in life, which gave them meaning and an orientation towards the future.

Schumacher wrote to his wife of his vision of a new

Europe, beginning in England, and his personal role in that future. After the war, he fulfilled this vision through his work as an economist for the government. But Schumacher's vision on social policy was something very different to the norm. In a public lecture he gave in 1948, Schumacher spoke about our need to move from a focus on purely economic measurements of progress to markers which include more human values. He described a human being's task as twofold: firstly to 'fully develop oneself', and secondly 'to form one's relationships to other people – family, groups, one's countrymen, mankind – sensibly, ethically, or expressed quite simply, with joy'.

Schumacher became a popular thought leader. Not only did he not shy away from using such terms as 'ethical', 'spiritual' and 'metaphysical' in his writings on economics, but he also owned one of the first houses in the UK to have solar panels installed on the roof. He championed organic farming methods, and the protection of the earth's resources as its 'natural capital'.

Although originally an atheist, Schumacher was an avid reader of books on comparative religion. He also learned to meditate. Gradually, he came to give up his atheistic beliefs and to admit to the possibility of a 'higher order of Being'.

In 1955, Schumacher took a three-month sabbatical to work for the government of the Union of Burma.

There he began to develop new ideas on matching economic policies to a culture and its values, saying that the materialistic consumption of the West's economics should not be imported to the people of Burma. Instead, he recommended a system of Buddhist economics, based on a respect for the dignity of meaningful work and the Buddhist values of purifying oneself through work as a spiritual practise. Over this period of his life, Schumacher began to recognise a 'vertical' perspective to life and an order of differing layers of consciousness up to a supreme consciousness or being. Just six years before his death at the early age of sixty-nine, Schumacher was received into the Roman Catholic Church.

Schumacher became famous for his book *Small Is Beautiful: A Study of Economics as if People Mattered*, which proposed the breaking up of large institutions into smaller parts. He could see that we were living beyond our means on earth, using up its natural capital. He recommended that every community should be self-sufficient, creating lots of small autonomous units. His book became a global bestseller, catching the zeitgeist of his day. Even since his death in 1977, Schumacher's value-centred economic policies continue to have a global following.

'Our task is to look at the world and see it whole.'
– E.F. Schumacher

Such a gestalt, whole-making perspective on the world requires a change in our habitual patterns of thinking, which won't come easily. The population of every country has unconscious collective beliefs about how they view themselves in relation to others. These include, for example, seeing ourselves as either one of many, or in competition with one another; and the perception of material wealth as a sign of achievement, or an indicator of spiritual poverty. Some of us may be willing to opt out of the capitalist race – as long as others do too. We can be happy with less as long as others have less too. It is the fear of falling behind or leaving our children at a disadvantage that makes us hesitate. If we are to have any chance of expanding the values on which we base our laws and economics, it will require the courage and leadership of individuals who are willing to speak plainly about noetic matters.

'Truth always rests with the minority, and the minority is always stronger than the majority, because the minority is generally formed by those who really have an opinion, while the strength of a majority is illusory, formed by the gangs who have no opinion – and who, therefore, in the next instant (when it is evident that the minority is the stronger) assume its opinion . . . while truth again reverts to a new minority.'

– Søren Kierkegaard, philosopher

A government cannot teach values to a population, but it is in the unique position of being able to allocate resources on behalf of the whole. A government spends and legislates according to what it values most. It can rethink a country's vision of what progress might be – to include measures of new values and both the vertical and horizontal life planes. What we honour, as Aristotle said, will be cultivated.

As traditional jobs are replaced by technology, we will need leadership that sees the dangers of a population with too much of the spare time we always wanted. Only a spiritual understanding of ourselves will see this to be the threat to our wellbeing that it is, and the volatility which might follow. But as we said earlier, the advancement of artificial intelligence (AI) will highlight what it is that really makes us human – that which is irreplaceable by machine. We will need to steer society towards this space, to invent new occupations based on these uniquely human aspects of ourselves.

AI is arriving to us in a period when the lower levels of Abraham Maslow's hierarchy of needs have been fulfilled for most, but by no means all of us, in Western society, and we might begin a new phase of human development. As the physical body becomes increasingly less necessary for manual labour, it is possible in future generations that our innate need to do and become will focus our attention on the spiritual self; towards self-actualisation and higher levels of Being. Suddenly, the theories of an Omega Point – the point of a gathering collective consciousness proposed by Teilhard de Chardin (which we will come to later) – no longer seem so farfetched. Not since the industrial revolution will society have seen such a rapid change in how we live. The simultaneous depletion of earth's natural resources will tame us to live within our means, to live as visitors on, rather than masters of, the planet. The governments of the near future will need the wisdom of philosophers and spiritual teachers, alongside economists, to steer a course towards a future whose vibrations we can already feel coming down the tracks.

In Ireland, we are privileged to have a President who has been both a politician and a poet. His ability to intertwine the different ways of seeing – the rational and intuitive mind – make him uniquely placed to speak on the importance of integrating these strands into the fabric of society. He kindly offered these thoughts on the concept of the Seven-Day Soul:

> *It is my firm belief that it is possible, indeed desirable, to cultivate one's particular cultural and spiritual identity while also cultivating reason, freedom of thought and independent enquiry.*
>
> *The cold reason of Descartes is insufficient, and utilising it in any way that quenches the music of*

the heart leaves us lesser human beings. The impulse for and pursuit of transcendent wonder does not require binary choices, such as a choice between reason and wonder.

In my work I have argued that we must, as individuals and as a society, strive for liberty and justice, as important ends in themselves, but also as values that bind all of the inhabitants of the world together, in their common humanity.

As we, together, seek new solutions and responses to the challenges facing humanity, we are invited to explore the necessary connections between economy, ecology and ethics. We do so, conscious that we live in a society that lacks a single, homogeneous and uncontested moral authority, but in which the pursuit of 'the common good' must necessarily be the subject of negotiation and deliberation, in a framework of respect for difference and diversity.

Our spirituality can be one of the sources we turn to when seeking the moral foundations for the ethical and deliberative society we wish to construct. That many, for example, are moved by the words and examples of the texts regarded as sacred, means that in addition to the claims for false certainties, a great source of danger, there is also the seeds for sustaining hope.

Our future together depends on the strength of moral foundations, and the extent to which they animate the network of integrating and mediating social structures that support the empowerment of ethical, informed and active citizens, constantly renewed by the wonder of being in the world.

**– An t-Uachtarán na hÉireann,
President Michael D Higgins**

15

Spirituality in Healthcare

Bone-Deep Peace

'A sad soul can kill ya quicker than a germ.'
 – John Steinbeck

So often we think of spirituality as being about beliefs. But it is really about how we see the world, and how we place ourselves in relation to everything else. It is no surprise then that spirituality, being about our very existence, was for centuries an integral part of healthcare. But over the past century, with improvements in technology, the spiritual aspect of care was relegated to the history books.

In part this was due to the enormous benefits brought by technology, and the advent of antibiotics – breakthroughs way beyond what had been achieved ever before. As a means of cure, spirituality could certainly not compete with the new regime of medicine which we now benefit from. But in more recent years, interest in spirituality as a means of healing is on the increase.

We have tended to use the words 'curing' and 'healing' interchangeably, but they contain subtle differences in meaning. Curing generally relates to a return to physical wellbeing.

Healing, on the other hand, can also imply an improvement in physical health, but also suggests a return to health or balance in the spiritual or psychological sense. Thus it is possible to be cured but not healed, just as it is possible to be healed but not cured. Our healthcare would benefit from an understanding of these subtle differences. Studies (see bibliography) have shown that it is possible to differentiate between spiritual wellbeing and both physical and mental wellbeing. This demonstrates that spiritual wellbeing is a separate aspect of health.

In an era of extraordinary technological advancement, we have all become shy about speaking of our spiritual needs to medical professionals. We tend to keep information on our spiritual practises to ourselves. But research shows that millions of dollars is being spent on complementary and alternative medicine (CAM) outside of mainstream medicine. It seems that CAM practitioners have become our modern-day shamans. Not all CAM practises are spiritual, of course, and each of us will differ on what we consider to be a spiritual treatment. But as research in this area has improved, and CAM practises have been shown to benefit the healing and sometimes curing process, the medical profession is beginning to reconnect with this lost aspect of healthcare.

In recent years, medical training programmes around the world have begun to include a training module on spirituality and its relevance to healthcare. At the very least, members of the medical profession need to be made aware of the effects of a patient's religious or spiritual beliefs on adhering to medication and end-of-life care and religious teachings on specific medical procedures. But if spiritual care has been shown to impact all dimensions of the person, physical, emotional and social, then it should not be seen as some fluffy add-on to the 'real' job of medicine. Just as employers have been forced through legislation to look after the psychological as well as physical welfare of the employee, the spiritual needs of the patient now need to be considered.

There may come a time when ignoring spiritual care will be seen to be negligent. Spiritual healthcare might then become the responsibility of the medical team; a valued part of the treatment plan, rather than an option for those who might be interested. Including the spiritual wellbeing of a patient in a treatment plan should be dependent on the wishes of the patient, and the relevance of spiritual wellbeing to treatment outcomes. It should not be influenced by the personal interests of the doctor.

Time is one of the main barriers that physicians report to looking after a patient's spiritual needs. Compassion comes from the word 'to be with', and as such it requires time and presence. It also demands much more of the real person attending the patient, below the garb of their role, so that they can relate human to human. Not every health professional is willing or able to do this, and to practise authentic, person-to-person compassionate presence with every patient requires a lot of training in self-care.

Hospital chaplaincy training programmes train religious and non-religious people to tend to patients' spiritual needs. This is a role that members of all the religious orders have undertaken for centuries, but in modern hospital care, it is only specific religious sacraments that are reserved for the religiously trained members of the hospital chaplaincy team. For some, the role of the hospital chaplain may simply mean staying with a patient, holding their hand or chatting to someone in need of company. For others, it might mean creating the space for them to verbalise the big existential questions about life after death, the meaning of their life, and the existence of God.

Although these seem to be big unanswerable questions, and many of them are, it can be the simple act of being with the person as they work through them that can offer healing. Sometimes patients feel they cannot speak about these issues to their family for fear of upsetting them, and even terminally ill children have been known to keep such questions away from their parents to protect them from further emotional pain.

When a patient struggles with leaving their children after their death, or with questions around their legacy, practical solutions like recording video legacies may help to ease the burden. Offering to speak with the family on a patient's behalf can help, as can introducing creative activities to ease suffering, or assisting patients to take up a creative hobby which they had once enjoyed. These types of activities not only help to lift the mood of the person, they can also help with feeling whole again, by revisiting what they enjoyed when they were being authentically themselves, outside of the role of 'patient'. This recognition of the part of the person that is not ill is recognised, and they are reminded that they still belong in the picture of all things. This is the reintegrative nature of spirituality – the making whole again.

Another reason for the slow reintroduction of spirituality into healthcare is the difficulty in arriving at a definition that includes all its aspects for everyone. Spirituality is deeply rooted in culture, but is also personal; it is an integral aspect of religion, but can also be considered apart from religion. This has meant that researchers in spirituality have had to take or make their own definition of spirituality for the purposes of their research; which in turn means that their findings cannot be generalised to apply to everyone or to all cultures. This makes it very difficult for the study of spirituality to achieve the quantity of evidence required to mainstream spirituality into the category of 'evidence-based medicine'.

Despite these research challenges, what has become clear is that spirituality includes experiences in four domains: intrapersonal, interpersonal, environmental, and transcendental.

* **Intrapersonal dimension**: refers to the within; how we feel in ourselves, our sense of our place in the world, our self-knowledge, and whether we view ourselves as being part of something divine.

* **Interpersonal dimension**: refers to the without; to what extent we use love in all its guises in our day-to-day lives, and our seven pillars in our interactions with others.

* **Environmental dimension**: reflects our sense of connection with nature, and our sense of awe, appreciation, and wonder about the world.

* **Transcendental dimension**: refers to our beliefs in a higher power and a divine order to life. It includes any understanding of ourselves as being from or of God, and our spiritual

practises, such as prayer, meditation, and religious celebrations.

We are all different as to how much we relate to these four dimensions of spirituality – some of us will be easily able to relate to all of them, and others perhaps to none, or just one. But these broad categories help researchers to catch those aspects of people's lives which, particularly in the Judeo-Christian traditions, might not necessarily have been considered spiritual.

In previous generations, connections with the land, and living and eating in accordance with the seasons, would have been so automatic that most of those generations would never have termed it 'spiritual'. On the other hand, many people today would describe themselves as deeply spiritual, but would have no belief in a transcendent reality. These different ways of experiencing a spiritual life gives us options on how we might raise spiritual conversations that include everyone, whether in the hospital, the workplace, public life or the home.

When 'All of Me Is Wrong': Total Pain

In her school days, Dame Cicely Saunders was a six-foot-tall, shy and intelligent girl who always felt a bit of an outsider. It was this feeling of not belonging that she later said helped her to relate to other people's suffering, and which ultimately led to her founding what we now know as the hospice movement.

Saunders was born into a wealthy British family in 1918. After leaving school, she wanted to study nursing, but due to family pressure, she instead went to study philosophy, politics and economics at Oxford. When war broke out in 1939, in just her first year of study, Saunders felt that she was not doing enough. She eventually went to study her first love of nursing, despite family opposition. Not long after she qualified, Saunders was told she would not be able to continue nursing because of a pre-existing back problem. She decided to train as a 'lady almoner', or what we would now call a medical social worker, in order to be able to continue her work with patients. At the same time, she completed her original studies at Oxford.

While working as a lady almoner, Saunders noticed that hospitals were not well equipped to deal with people who were terminally ill or dying. She began to develop her ideas for a better care system for these patients. She became particularly close to one Polish patient by the name of David Tasma, who had terminal cancer. He had lost his original Jewish faith, and felt that his life had been worthless. Over the course of his final month of life, Saunders talked with David regularly about the meaning of life, and helped him return to his lost faith tradition.

Saunders increasingly noticed the multifaceted nature of pain in her patients, the relevance of emotional and spiritual matters to suffering, and the pain relief that can come from working through these issues. When she spoke about her ideas to a Harley Street surgeon she worked with, he told her that her ideas were good, but that she would get nowhere in progressing them unless she became a doctor herself. Not a woman to shy away from a challenge, Saunders went on to train as a doctor.

During her hospital training, Saunders researched pain medication for the dying. At that time, doctors were slow to give morphine to patients because of the risk of developing dependency. Patients were often left in agony, as the tide of thought of the day was to delay the administration of pain medications for as long as possible. Photographing and documenting patients on their arrival and again a few days later, when they'd had proper pain relief and pain prevention, Saunders gathered evidence of patients who were now able to engage in conversations, and return to activities within the hospital setting which they could still enjoy. Patients, relieved of the all-encompassing burden of pain, were freed to become more of themselves again. For Saunders, vital signs of life in the terminally ill patient were, in her own words, 'the hand steady enough to draw, the mind alert enough to write poems and to play cards, and above all, the spirit to enjoy family and spend the last weekends at home'.

Saunders wrote extensively on the importance of acknowledging the spiritual dimension of the patient, the person's personal narrative, the value of listening to their story, and understanding the multiple layers which contribute to a person's suffering. Looking at pain in this way was a means to revealing additional problems beneath the obvious physical pain, layers which might require many different approaches to resolve. Pain, in Saunders' new model, was indivisible from the whole of the person.

In 1969, she introduced the new concept of 'total pain' into the medical vocabulary. Total pain encompasses all of the physical, emotional, social, and spiritual distress of the patient, which culminates in the overall level of experienced pain. In one of her papers, Saunders described a conversation with a patient by the name of Mrs Henson:

> Well, doctor, the pain began in my back but now it seems that all of me is wrong.' Mrs Henson went on to perfectly but unknowingly describe her own total pain as she explained her concerns for her husband and son and the financial cost of them missing work to look after her. She spoke about her desperate need for more pain medication and the feeling that no one understood. Until after a pause, she said, 'But it's so wonderful to begin to feel safe again.

Without realising it, Mrs Henson had addressed her own physical pain, her social worries about her family and her spiritual need for security and peace.

During her medical training, Saunders, helped by a small group of like-minded colleagues, proposed the need for a dedicated hospital for the terminally ill. In 1967, St Christopher's Hospice, London – the first of its kind in the world – opened its doors to its first patient. The hospice movement was born.

SPINE: Our Axis of Integration

Psycho-neuro-immuno-endocrinology (PNIE) is a relatively recent direction in medical research, which has developed over the past few decades. It is the study of the links between the mind and the body, the interactions between psychology and the nervous, immune and endocrine systems.

Several PNIE studies have focused on the effects of stress on the immune and neuro-endocrine systems, showing how different types, durations and severity of psychological stressors affect the functions of these systems of the body. In the other direction, sickness in one of these systems can cause psychological changes in mood, alertness, and sleeping patterns.

Although spiritual wellbeing has been shown to be able to stand as a separate type of wellbeing, it is deeply connected to physical, emotional and social wellness. It is probably only a matter of time before PNIE becomes SPINE – the spiritual-psycho-immuno-neuro-endocrine axis of the body. Participation in regular religious practises has been shown to extend life expectancy, decrease pain and improve coping (see bibliography for these studies).

A sense of fulfilment of life goals and feeling that we have had a meaningful existence is related to improved quality of life for patients with advanced disease. A study by the American Pain Society found that prayer was the most commonly used non-drug method of pain relief among hospital patients, with 76 per cent making use of it. Spirituality is also associated with improved recovery times, and improved physical functioning following surgery; and although spirituality is a separate dimension of wellbeing, many of the benefits of spiritual practises make themselves visible through better physical and emotional functioning.

For years, the placebo response – whereby a patient finds benefit in a 'fake pill' – has been thought to be due to the effects of belief on the body. 'Faith healings' were associated with this power of belief, too, although how it might work has never been fully understood. Some have suggested that the placebo response should be renamed the meaning response, on the basis that the placebo response works when a person is able to find meaning or make sense of a situation in some way.

Viktor Frankl and Cicely Saunders would agree with this view. Both these giant thought leaders wrote about the importance of finding meaning in our suffering. But for Frankl, spiritual problems and existential questions should not be pathologised, or seen as problems, but as a sign of accomplishment – a sign that a person has achieved a certain level of thoughtfulness. When we find meaning in our suffering, or view our search for meaning as a personal achievement in itself, the pain-reducing interactions of SPINE are set in motion.

> **'To be religious is to have found an answer to the question "What is the meaning of life?"'**
>
> **– Albert Einstein**

Spiritual Dissonance

Each of us has different ways of coping with illness, and these ways may vary at different stages of our life. It's important that finding meaning is not loaded on as another burden on the already stretched resources of a patient. Too easily, even the best intended actions can add to the psychological load of someone who is ill. The pressure to wave one's wig in the air in defiance of cancer can seem very far removed from the actual feelings of the cancer patient. The mind-over-matter philosophy can unintentionally add further layers of guilt to someone who feels that they should be able to 'think' themselves well.

Spiritual dissonance is the psychological term used to describe a disharmony between one's authentic spiritual self or beliefs and one's actions. Like cognitive dissonance (when we do something that is not in keeping with our beliefs, or hold two or more conflicting beliefs on a subject), spiritual dissonance results in feelings of hollowness, living by someone else's script, and becoming 'un-selved'.

When a medical team takes a spiritual history of a patient, they take the first steps to avoiding spiritual dissonance and increasing the possibility of successful treatment. When we know the religious and/or spiritual beliefs of a patient, we can work alongside their needs, and address any potential conflicts as early as possible. For example, in some faiths, times of day or religious festivals may affect the timing of medications and this needs to be taken into account.

A strong connection to the environment can be used to help with pain and coping if it is in keeping with the spiritual life of the individual. Dealing early with beliefs around the afterlife and being sick as a 'divine punishment', can help to lessen the negative consequences of such beliefs. But the medical team needs to tread carefully in challenging religious beliefs. In these kinds of situations, they can offer scientific explanations of disease but they cannot negate the faith of the patient. It can be a difficult line to tread.

Research shows that most patients would like their spiritual beliefs to be considered in treatment. Studies also show that the majority of healthcare professionals are also happy to harness the potential benefits.

These benefits extend beyond the patient, to include improved wellbeing in the healthcare workers treating the patient, because their work increases in meaning when they care for patients in this more holistic way.

Although spirituality is looking likely to be a promising new growth area of healthcare, there is much to be done and a long way to go before we truly internalise its benefits in our model of wellbeing. The healthcare profession would do well to take its lead from the people they serve.

Pat Caslin, who lives with MS, spoke about the possibility for wellness in illness, during a talk to doctors at St James' Hospital, Dublin.

I have multiple sclerosis [MS] for ten years. About four years ago it became 'secondary progressive'. In that period, I've come to dislike the term ill-health. Ill-health suggests that illness and health are flipsides of the same coin; or that they are on some sort of continuum, where there's good health over here, over there you're seriously chronically ill or nearly dead. So as you dial up the illness, you dial down the health.

I have a different view. I think health and illness are not flipsides of the same coin. You can see them in different dimensions. I'm chronically ill. Yet I consider myself very healthy. Health to me is a state of mind. It's about wellbeing. It's about the reasons that you wish to be alive. It's about your optimism. It's about your view of your future and the things you can do.

There's loads of things that I can't do. I used to play golf. I used to cycle. I can't do them now. But I don't want to do anything that I can't do. I'm very happy doing the things that I can. I suppose I'm lucky. I'm cerebral. I think a lot and I read a lot. I'm fortunate that I can still do those things.

Life requires more planning when you have a chronic illness, particularly when your legs don't work. Simple things like, when you bend down to tie your shoelaces, you wonder, Is there anything else I should be doing while I'm down here?

Health and wellbeing also involve trade-offs. I've lost a lot of tone in the muscles of my legs, and I have a lot of spasticity. I can take drugs for it, but they upset my stomach. I can take drugs that help me walk a bit better, but they upset my stomach as well. My trade-offs are: I don't take the drugs, because my wellbeing is more compromised by feeling upset or sick than by not being able to walk. I don't do things that compromise my wellbeing.

What's the importance of that? The importance of that is that it allows me to be positive. Positivity is really important, because if you're not positive, well then, it's difficult to go out and engage with people. It's difficult to see a good future for yourself. It's difficult to participate socially. Being positive means that people want to be around you. If you're not positive – if you're giving out, you're complaining about your future, you want to be somewhere else, you want to be in a different situation – well, people aren't going to want to stay around you that long. And that will limit your ability to have a good outlook.

In all my consultations with my neurologists, there is probably only one that has focused on my wellbeing – the things that I want to do, giving me optimism and things to look forward to. Most of my consultations focus on my illness, and that is different.

I've had a lot of MS consultations. I've come to realise that some consultants are more open to questions, and some of them are less. I used to feel a little short-changed when my appointment was with a clinical nurse specialist and I didn't get to see the consultant. But I've come to realise that probably my best consultations are where I have time with the clinical nurse specialist. I have time to ask all my questions. I have time to sort out what's important and what's not important, and then a small amount of time with the consultant afterwards, to deal with the important questions, when I'm clear on what's relevant and what's not.

That style of consultation has been very valuable

for me. Patients need time to process what's being said to them, and they need somebody that can allow them to clear their minds, so that they can absorb and internalise and focus on the important things that are going to help them recover.

I went to see a neurology specialist in the US about four years ago. I wanted to get an opinion on my progression. I asked him, 'What's my progression likely to be?' He said, 'You have a progressive disease and progressive diseases progress.' I left there thinking, 'Is he holding back on me? Is he being nice to me?' I felt I hadn't got great value from that answer to my question.

Except afterwards I thought about it and I said, 'I'm glad he didn't give me a sense of what the progression was.' Because if he gave me a scenario of progression that he thought most likely, that would have become my own narrative. It would have become what I believed would happen, and that would have got into my subconscious, and it would have become self-fulfilling. That, I think, could have been very, very dangerous.

Instead, this specialist allowed me to choose my own outlook, my own narrative as to what my disease progression would be. That allowed me then to decide on my own reality as to what my MS would be. I think that's important, because I think if he focused on a particular progression or a particular outcome, it's really easy for that to become your future. We create our own realities. We don't see life as it is, we see life as we are. What goes on in your head is really important to what happens you. That is really important. You've got to set your expectations high.

When you're giving bad news, before you speak, three questions you might think about asking yourself: 'Does this need to be said? Does this need to be said by me? Does this need to be said by me now?' Particularly, if you have really bad news to give, if there's terminal illness involved.

How a doctor communicates with patients, and how a patient perceives their doctor's sense of his or her wellbeing, is important as well. Allowing room for patients to have positivity, even in the face of difficult outlooks, is something that I think is really, really important, because positivity is what keeps me going.

Neurotheology

The effects of spirituality on the brain and on health are difficult to measure because spirituality is, by its very nature, personal, subjective and relational. Over recent decades, there has been an increasing use of brain-scanning techniques, such as fMRI, to look inside the brain to see what is happening when someone prays, meditates, or reports to be having a spiritual experience.

Mindfulness meditation went mainstream when its proponents were able to present research that showed physical changes in the brains of participants before and after a mindfulness programme. It is thanks to these types of studies that mindfulness has become so accepted in mainstream medicine and psychology. But researchers are at pains to say that all meditation is not alike. There are thousands of different types of meditation taught across the globe, with different practises, different expectations, different goals and different outcomes. But what is certain is that what we do repeatedly, we become.

Religious and spiritual practises have also been studied using all the various neurological tests, such as fMRI, PET scans, SPECT, EEG, and psychological tests. However, it could be argued that spirituality has to be the 'and then some' of all these computations. When researchers ask practitioners about what they felt, saw and thought, they are really only collecting the corresponding *biology* of the experiences. Following this line of thought, to some extent the only way to isolate measurements of the purely spiritual would be to focus our attention on what is left when we ignore the biological and psychological measurements. Only then, it might be said, can we get to the 'truly' spiritual – separate from the results of our biology.

But to take this approach would mean that we are looking upon our spirituality as being separable from the body and mind, like the slices of pie idea. An alternative metaphor might be to view spirituality as a painter's canvas, on which is drawn the body and mind. Spirit in this case is the ground of our being.

Spiritual meditation and prayer practises usually require the person to narrow their focus or their attention on a mantra, a sacred word, a visual point, or the breath. These practises produce increased activity in what is known as the prefrontal lobes to the front of the brain, behind the forehead. This kind of brain activity is also seen with non-spiritual or religious practises, such as a meditation to improve mental focus.

Prefrontal brain activation reduces the processing of sensory information in the parietal lobe, that part of the brain responsible for giving us our sense of orientation in relation to our surroundings. Scientists believe it is this deactivation of the parietal lobe that causes the feelings of being spacey, floating, and out of our body, and also the loss of the sense of time passing, as these spatio-temporal senses are normally processed by the parietal lobe. These effects are also common in hypnosis.

Mystical experiences in meditation seem to involve some activation of the circuitry of the entire brain, which reflects the idea of the 'wholeness' concept of spirituality – the coming together of the typically logical, narrow-focused left brain and the more instinctual, abstract right hemisphere. However, there are some neurological differences in brain functioning between spiritual and non-spiritual practises which reflect the differences in the meditator's focus inward or towards an external deity.

In a religious prayer or meditation, the individual is normally thinking of a higher power either outside or within themselves, rather than focusing on their everyday personas, and this difference shows up in fMRI measurements. Similarly, in any practise, if it requires the individual to mentally repeat a mantra or phrase, or requires movement, such as in yoga, then this will also be reflected in the neurological scans.

The fact that research has shown particular patterns of neural activity in the brain during meditation and prayer doesn't mean that these patterns cause the spiritual feelings – i.e., that sensations of being in the presence of God is nothing more than an effect of our neurological processes. In scientific studies, researchers are very careful to differentiate between cause and correlation; what they study and the methods they use will depend on which of these they hope to identify. In many cases, it is not possible to say that one thing causes another, but only that two things are related to each other (correlation).

Alternatively, we could assume that the changes do indeed cause the spiritual sensations; but we could not then tell if these neural patterns allowed the person to perceive the world more clearly, as it really is, or to simply feel *as if* they perceive more clearly – as if they are one with the universe or God. Are we measuring spiritual experiences, or are we measuring spiritual sensations? How each of us answers this question is a matter of personal opinion. The ultimate answer is far beyond what we yet know.

On Reflection

As a patient

Ask yourself, which of the four domains of spirituality – Intrapersonal, Interpersonal, Environmental and Transcendental – do you feel most describe your spiritual life? Perhaps only one does; or perhaps you experience aspects of them all. How might you introduce more of these dimensions into your days? Are there other patients who might enjoy a chat on the subject? While you might think that speaking about spirituality will make your loved ones worry about you, you can explain how you see it as a way back to healing. Family and loved ones can feel very powerless. Inviting them to talk to you about these matters offers them a way to feel useful. If you don't feel that you can bring up spiritual matters with them, ask your treatment team if there are hospital chaplains who you can talk to.

As a family member or friend of a patient

Firstly, you have to look after yourself, so the question above also applies in your self-care. Secondly, people can be nervous about bringing up spiritual vocabulary, out of concern that it might frighten the patient, or make them feel they are talking about dying when this is not intended. What do you know about the person that might give you a clue as to how they experience spirituality, if you feel you cannot ask? How might you bring alternative ways for the patient to experience spirituality, if some are no longer an option? For example, a patient who loved to experience awe of nature and the wilderness but is now bed-bound might again tap into awe by watching a nature documentary with you. Someone else might love the lift that a group of visitors can bring.

As a healthcare worker

Practise taking a spiritual history where appropriate; ask your patient or client about when, how and where they might experience the spiritual, and their wishes about incorporating it into treatment. Many people think spirituality and religion in healthcare is only for the dying. It's important to be able to explain how spirituality is part of everyone's wellbeing and impacts on our overall health. You may want to pre-prepare a few sentences that you could use to open a space in the conversation for your patient to speak about their spiritual health. Can you name the four dimensions of spirituality and give examples of each one? This might be a good place to begin.

16

The Spirit of Our Spaces

Social Myopia and a Prescription for Alpine Air

'I call architecture frozen music.'

— **Goethe**

Some words become so everyday to us that we forget what they actually mean. Take 'apartment living', for example; was it someone's original intention to 'viralise' the plague of loneliness that is now so much a part of modern life? Did they really plan to keep people 'apart'? Despite the rise in the number of people gathered in physical proximity in cities throughout the world, feelings of isolation and discontent are on the rise as so many of us are forced to move away from family and the community in which we were raised, in search of work. This disconnected-style living makes it increasingly difficult for those who have had to move away to get past a superficial level of friendship, and almost impossible to regain the rootedness of tribe.

Social isolation is a major risk factor for many

illnesses. Studies have shown that growing up in a city doubles the chances of someone developing schizophrenia, and also increases vulnerability to other mental health disorders, such as depression and anxiety. Belonging to a lower socio-economic group is also linked to an increase in health problems, including coronary heart disease, although some research has shown that these risks are reduced when there are more green areas available. Where it is the environment or a lack in the environment that causes these disorders, they become noetic illnesses – symptoms of living without regard for our membership in nature. There is a balance to be made between our dual needs for physical space and social connectedness – our need for short-and long-lens vision, both literal and metaphorical.

> '**Look deep into nature and then you will understand everything better.**'
>
> **– Albert Einstein**

Neuro-architecture is the study of how architecture affects the human brain. Researchers in the area are providing insights into just how much our streetscapes affect us. Our moods, thoughts and behaviour are intimately connected, so it is really important that each of us becomes architecturally aware and streetscape-savvy. If the journey home is as visually enclosed as the office we left, if we are never in touching distance of greenery, or the soundscape we live in is never silent, then we become far more likely to be irritable and depressed. As the majority of the population is unaware of how our surroundings affect us and our noetic needs, then we may mistakenly put our low states down to general tiredness after a day's work, and do nothing to remedy it. Becoming conscious of the effects of the larger context that we live in is key not only to a healthier, but also more spiritually meaningful, life. We do not exist in miniature universes, separate from the rest of nature or each other, but affect and are affected by the whole.

Researchers in neuro-architecture use biological measurements to demonstrate the effects of our surroundings on the brain and body. Using apps and wearable devices that measure skin conductance (a measure of arousal), and electroencephalogram headsets that measure brain activity, the researchers have shown amazing effects on the mind and body that we are not consciously aware of. One such study showed that a person's physiology changed depending on whether or not the façade of a building was monotonous or interesting.

A busy, interesting city streetscape engages us and lifts our mood. The same has been found for residential streetscapes. The hippocampus is a part of the brain responsible for visual-spatial awareness, and it is cells in this area of the brain which are affected by our environment. The brains of London taxi drivers also have increased connectivity in the hippocampus. As cab drivers repeatedly map their way around the city, mentally working out their route and then physically making their way from one point to the next, they physically change their brain. Off the west coast of Thailand, children of the Moken fishing tribe are able to see underwater at depths far deeper than normal for most humans. The pupils of their eyes have adapted to constrict to a degree never seen before in humans, while the lens of their eyes also changes shape in a similar way to dolphins and seals, allowing them to see at underwater depths at which most of us would be blind. What we do, we become, and what we surround ourselves with affects what we do, in a never-ending cycle that we would do well to take notice of.

> **'We shape our buildings, afterwards our buildings shape us.'**
> **– Winston Churchill, 1943**

Good architecture and planning is as much about building as it is about not building, about the effects of space and enclosure. The inclusion of green areas gives people a place to gather, but that space must be neither too big nor too small, with just the right amount of amenities to fill it, to move people gently towards each other and avoid feelings of being exposed.

This principle is as relevant to a workspace as it is to city planning. Large, extravagant foyers in new office buildings can often have the unintended effect of making people feel exposed and anxious. The Pruitt-Igoe housing complex in St Louis, USA – which had thirty-three featureless apartment blocks became notorious for criminality and social dysfunction. Critics argued that the wide open spaces between the blocks – presumably intended to provide recreational space – actually discouraged a sense of community. We do not like to wander into vastly open spaces where we feel 'watched' by what surrounds us. In both large, open-plan office foyers and the wide spaces between apartment blocks, the feeling of exposure probably hits on a primal nerve in our biology, which warns us that being exposed is dangerous. From an evolutionary perspective, it certainly was.

Rachel and Stephen Kaplan are psychologists at the University of Michigan, USA, who discovered the restorative effects on our thinking of being in nature. Their finding that people concentrate better after spending time in nature inspired many other studies into the effects of nature on our being. Nature, they found, offered us 'soft fascinations' that we can engage with using effortless attention. When we do so, we rest the more effort-full, focused attention that we normally use.

The discovery of what the Kaplans called 'attention

restoration' through nature led to later research showing that being in nature also lowers blood pressure, improves reaction times, decreases anxiety during recovery from surgery, improves attendance at school and work, reduces inflammation, improves short-term memory, results in a reduction in the risk of children developing short-sightedness (myopia), and increases feelings of awe.

While some of these studies did include forest walks, other studies used the introduction of some plants into an office space, or the simplest snippets of nature that can be found in urban areas. There are times in our lives when we seem to instinctively return to nature. When someone is sick we bring flowers, as we do at funerals and at births – unconsciously hooking ourselves back into the natural world.

As research into the effects of spaces on our psychological health expands, it is perhaps time to move ourselves further towards the pinnacle of Maslow's hierarchy of needs. While we have learned the extent to which the spaces we live in affect us in a perpetual cycle of life, we need to aim to build our buildings, towns and homes with our highest needs in mind – those of self-transcendence, unity and the value-driven life. Good design can speak to all four dimensions of our spirituality – our inner life, our interpersonal life, the environmental, and the transcendental.

Every scene we enter, every space we walk into,

has a corresponding script. This script informs our behaviours and experiences in that space: we become silent in a chapel, and chatty at a party; we take off our shoes in a pristine white space, and we tend to lose track of time in a clock-less shopping centre.

Designing spiritual spaces means creating spaces whose script brings us the stillness of our vertical life plane, where we can take time out from our endless doing and cluttering, to simply be; spaces that encourage us to contemplate something greater, be that God, nature, our higher selves, or all of existence. Our buildings as much as our spaces can meet our most basic needs for safety, freeing us to love by freeing us from fear. Spaces can move us gently towards each other, or they can separate us. They can be monuments of gratitude to the environment for the materials she gives us, and embodiments of beauty when we build with respect of our surroundings. A building can either say that we are conquerors of our environment, or slip humbly in to place to watch nature's grand show.

When we look at our environment from this perspective, acknowledging the ability of design to lift us towards our highest potential, is not so much a luxury as a responsibility. If our spaces can animate us in the way research has shown, then every building we build, every space we create, should reflect within it the vertical and horizontal life planes of reflection and animation towards our better selves.

It would be easy for us to sit back in resignation,

and leave it up to the town planners and architects of the world to provide the design required by our noetic needs. But our spiritual landscape is made up of many different kinds of spaces. A special chair, altar, yoga mat, garden, window box, noticeboard, side table, religious symbol, meeting room, pond, grave, mantelpiece, or shelf can become our spiritual space, our nudge towards our higher selves.

Even spaces of time can become our spiritual nourishment. We can choose to use our route to work as our morning prayer space, by actively choosing to show love in its different forms to everyone we meet along the way. We can do the same with a meeting room, so that every time we enter the room we are reminded to be patient, kind, and respectful of the highest potentials or inner divinity within everyone we speak to there.

We can collect images and items and display them on a shelf or corner of our desk, to act as personal reminders to live by our values. We might buy or collect books by writers and philosophers we respect and gather them on a shelf that we pass by frequently, re-reading them regularly as another way to repeatedly reconnect ourselves towards what we can be. We can write our Seven-Day Soul pillar on a slip of paper and prop it on a desk light, creating an altar to those values. We can display wall decals with inspirational quotes, or simply print out and display passages from books that inspire us to grow. We can make our car our chosen space by listening to inspirational podcasts while we drive, perhaps planning and reviewing the day with our highest values in mind.

Ask yourself for whom or for what might you light a lamp. This is a lovely way of introducing a spiritual message to children, perhaps allowing each of them to 'light' their own battery-operated tea light in front of their place at the table, while each of them says, 'I'm lighting a lamp for my friend who was out sick from school today/for Mum/for Dad, who is tired/for the people we learned about in school who are starving/ to say thanks for the food we eat/because I hope that we can stop hurting the environment/so that we can remember to stop hurting others/because geography class was cancelled today....'

In our home we have what we call the 'magic chair'. When the children were very young, we used the chair as a place where they could curl up or sit on our laps when they were upset, and everything would feel better. It still works its magic. It has pride of place in our kitchen, and for the last fifteen years or so it has been my meditation and prayer chair, a place to collapse into at the end of the day, a place to read inspirational authors in quietness in the very early morning or late evening, a place to cuddle with the children, and a place for the children to be safe and be still as they watch the busyness of life around them. It is often the only time that they will sit in one place and chat, giving us precious times of connection and togetherness that I am eternally grateful for. It is old and tatty, but is probably the greatest space of love in the house. As such, it is a very spiritual space, just a few feet wide.

We tend to think of spaces as being physical – as landscapes of some sort. But our spiritual spaces can use any of our senses and the more that are included, the more they can inspire us to remember our noetic life. Consider how your daily soundscape contributes towards or detracts from your attempts to live a more spiritual life. Is there a sound space in your day that helps you to connect to your vertical life plane of stillness? Do you get *any* silence in your day? Does the music you play on your phone or in your home prompt higher thoughts and aspirations in you? Do you ever listen to inspirational audiobooks while out walking the dog? Does relaxing music help you to practise patience with the kids or your partner? Do you speak to people who inspire you? Do you speak to your children about their spiritual needs?

What about your light-scape and sense-scape? Does clutter make you irritable and unable to move past your safety needs? Does your bedroom really feel restful so that you can serve others with patience the next day? Does soft lamp lighting or the fading sun slow you down towards stillness, at the end of a day of doing?

Could you create a loose change jar for a favourite

charity? Does your home reflect your highest values – such as family, God, the environment, love – or whatever your own values might be? Are there ways to introduce a little more of what's really important to you into your day?

Awakening Awe in Our Lives

The dictionary describes awe as 'a feeling of reverential respect mixed with fear and wonder'.

Awe is an emotion far out of fashion in our knowledge economy. We have little time for that which cannot be easily grasped, collated and branded. As we have already seen, society's collective lens has a preference for the concrete and immediate. Awe, on the other hand, opens up a window on the moment, takes us momentarily outside of time, expanding our view into the ineffable, making us feel our smallness in a cosmic lesson in humility. It is no coincidence that the word awe stems from the Norse word for 'terror'.

According to studies, two things happen when we experience awe:

1. We get a sense of vastness – we feel that we have perceived something vast in size, number, scope, pertinence, complexity or social relevance.

2. We are forced to move around our current picture of the world or beliefs about

something, in order to accommodate the experience.

Different moments will evoke awe for each of us. Religious and transcendent beliefs and experiences can give us a sense of our place in a greater plan, as can the enjoyment of art, music and nature. In these moments we become less impatient, more generous with our time, less materialistic, less automated and habitual in our behaviour, and more contented with life. But it is probably no coincidence that nature's ability to expand our sense of time is linked not only to awe, but also to a decrease in short-sightedness.

Expanding Our Lens on the World: Social Myopia?

There are now several studies which show that spending time in the outdoors lessens the likelihood of a child developing short-sightedness, or myopia. An Australian study of over 2,000 twelve-year-olds found that the children who spent more time outdoors, rather than playing sports indoors, had less chance of developing the disorder.

A Taiwanese study compared two nearby schools, encouraging one school to increase outdoor activity during break times, while the other continued as normal. The rate of myopia in the more outdoor school after a year was 8.41 per cent compared to 17.65 per cent in the indoor sports school. It seems that living life in built-up areas or mostly indoors, where there is little opportunity for our eyes to use long-sightedness, results in a reduced capacity to see long-sightedly. But what is really interesting is when we connect awe, vastness and long-sightedness. It takes a little leap, but it is not completely metaphorical.

Society's inability to value spirituality may partially come down to our indoor, phone-obsessed, short-lensed living. Unconsciously prompted by our environment, is it possible that we have become short-sighted in our collective unconscious, just as the eyes of the Moken children adapted to their underwater diving? Without the spaciousness of nature, or an understanding for our smallness, have we lost our ability to see further than the eye can see, to appreciate the history behind us, and the future before us; to appreciate the hidden, the Godly, the universal, and the cosmic, whose vastness is revealed only with a larger lens? Have we lost all capacity to appreciate that which should silence us in awe?

The great philosopher Plato was the first to speak of the relationship of everything within the whole, the relationship between the multiplicity of all life and the unity of the whole universe. For Plato, there existed a geometric code which is repeated over and over within everything in the natural universe. For centuries, these geometric shapes – based on the three basic patterns of the circle, the square and the triangle, and the overlaying of the three – have been handed down and included in sacred spaces and influential architecture around the world, across many different traditions, as a symbol of Plato's sacred geometry.

HRH Prince Charles has long been an advocate and thought leader in replacing humankind back within nature, rather than outside of it, to heal the separation which took place in our thinking, and then in our living, since the thirteenth century. Poundbury is a modern English town built in the early 1990s in accordance with Prince Charles' goal of creating towns that create a sense of community, built on the values of environmental sustainability and harmony with the surroundings. Poundbury was perhaps the first experimental town of its kind, but since then the philosophy of values-based social design has gained considerable momentum.

'Conscious Cities' is an international initiative which aims to use research findings to design cities that consciously and proactively benefit quality of life. By gathering data from psychology and the neurosciences about how we behave in cities, what helps and what harms us, the project aims to design urban spaces which respect our physical, mental and spiritual wellbeing – reducing the stresses of overly busy streetscapes, increasing playful learning for children, decreasing loneliness through design, and incorporating aspects that inspire awe, and which build communities that are healthier, more democratic and more inclusive.

Just as the pyramids were built to inspire awe, and monasteries to encourage contemplation, the

Conscious Cities initiative aims to change cities so that they in their turn will change us. The aim is to build 'healthscapes' that are people-centred; that respond, for example, in real time to overly busy streets by diverting traffic, or down-regulating flashing advertising billboards. Healthscapes prime curiosity in children on the journey to school, and change the mood of people at potential flashpoints, such as after football matches. While it might be hard to think of this increased automation of our living spaces as being spiritual, it is the very act of recognising the fluid, evolving, aspect of people that makes it so.

For some time, great cities and spaces have fallen victim to the celebrity factor of architecture, with buildings being designed for the wow factor – more for the benefit of the architect's ego than of humanity. But with what Prince Charles calls the 'grammar of harmony' we can move away from modern design's egoistic attempts to shock the senses, towards a more relational design, where the buildings and spaces that we live in resonate with something deeply unconscious in us; which in turn makes us feel that something is meant by our built environment.

As with the Conscious Cities project, we can build our surroundings to recognise the sacredness of ordinary, everyday life. In this way, our environments can remind us to choose to either direct our noses to the next firefight in our hectic lives, or to lift our lens to the bigger picture of things; to have a greater presence to life, or to the Greater Presence in life.

17
Transcendent Spirituality
The Un-Common Ground of World Religions

'There is only one religion, though there are a hundred versions of it.'

— George Bernard Shaw

Despite the downturn in membership of religious institutions, we have never lost the most human need for an answer to our ultimate concerns about our existence. Many of us still intuit that there is something more than the eye can see.

Spirituality is a path, not a place. It is the active integration of a way of life, and a realisation of something greater than ourselves, be that humanity, nature, or God. It can be a lonely road when undertaken without belonging to a large group with shared beliefs; it requires the individual to become active and thoughtful in their search, and to develop a deep understanding of the workings of their own mind. This is very different to knowing our own mind – in fact, it's almost the opposite. Few of us can recognise our own biases, predilections and omissions. But in order to come to a personally fulfilling spirituality, each of us must be allowed to take the time to challenge, doubt, explore and question all aspects of our spirituality, if we are to have any chance of maturing.

Every one of us needs the space to move away from social pressures to conform, and to be offered support and the safety to question, if we as a society are to reintegrate spirituality back into our picture of ourselves. If we succeed in doing so, we may finally be able to offer the healing that has been so elusive to those who need it. Spiritual maturity, existential understanding, and a renewed focus on values may well be the greatest animators towards the next great evolution of humankind. As all religions have taught for centuries, learning to care for others as ourselves, in self-transcendent acts of compassion, may just be the purpose of our lives.

The ultimate truth that we find must be true for all people, or it is not the final truth. Although there are indeed many ways to what millions call God, Atman, the Ground of Being, the Logos, Ultimate Mystery, Love, and the multitude of other names by which this is known, what we seek must in fact transcend the limitations of definition in order to be the Ultimate All.

But the mystery and unknowing that are inherent in this type of transcendence don't do well in Western culture. A politician who says they are undecided on a point is unlikely to be a politician for long. A strong opinion, no matter how unconsidered, wins the day. Strength and noise win out over consideration and reflection. We simply haven't been taught how to sit with not knowing in contemplation.

Spiritual seeking is a common thread that connects all the world religions with spiritual but not religious (SBNR) paths and secular spiritual practises. It is the rising to the surface of an unconscious, intuitive pull towards knowledge of, or union with, something greater than ourselves that transcends the apparent divide between religion and secularity.

Spirituality spans this gap more easily than religiosity. The more comprehensive any description is, the less comprehensible it will be, to paraphrase Viktor Frankl. It is highly likely that as world religions pull themselves slowly towards finding a shared voice, it will be the commonalities in the mystical teachings of each that will be easiest to find. In every tradition, the greatest mystics have all struggled to find words to describe feelings of being one with their deity or highest levels of consciousness. They all describe emotions such as oneness, unity, awe, wonder and love; and also, sometimes, experiences of an absolute absence, vastness and emptiness.

Thus it is relatively easy for different traditions to unite in the experiential aspect of spirituality. The difficulty will be in finding a way to unite the wordy dogma of the various theological teachings and practises without diluting any of them – unless each faith is willing to let go of their proprietary ownership of their teachings, in search of a common truth.

The Perennial Philosophy

At face value, the outer teachings of religions are clearly different: Christianity teaches God as a Trinity, Hinduism includes many Gods and Judaism teaches one God, while Buddhism is non-theistic. But at an esoteric, more metaphysical level, their teachings are more easily reconciled, as long as we take their teachings to be more symbolic than literal.

Aldous Huxley was a twentieth century English writer and philosopher who looked at the commonalities between all the major world faith traditions in his famous work *The Perennial Philosophy*. Abraham Maslow – who developed the hierarchy of needs discussed earlier – considered Huxley to be a 'transcender', who had reached the top of the hierarchy. (Maslow felt the same about Albert Einstein.)

After closely studying the teachings of all the main faith traditions, Huxley found four doctrines – the four common threads connecting them all – which he described as the 'perennial philosophy':

1. The phenomenal world of matter and of

individualised consciousness – the world of things, animals, human beings, and even gods – is the manifestation of a Divine Ground within which all partial realities have their being, and apart from which, they would all be non-existent; (i.e. all matter and species [including us] exist in a Divine Ground, and would not exist without it.)

2. Humans are capable of more than just knowing about this Divine Ground; they can also know it by direct intuition, which is superior to discursive reasoning. This immediate knowledge unites the knower with that which is known.

    It is through certain practises – including the spiritual practises we have discussed in this book – that we can unite with the Divine Ground. Most traditions teach that this is done through both our daily activities, and also contemplative practises.

    It is likely that it is this unitive feeling with the divine that churchgoers have felt lacking in religious services, and so have tried to find it themselves. In the Seven-Day Soul we bring together these practises in the vertical and horizontal life planes. Practise is more important than endless talking.

3. Human beings possess a double nature: a phenomenal ego (our sense of self as we know it) and an eternal self, which is the inner human, the spirit, the spark of divinity within the soul. It is possible for individual human beings, if they wish, to identify themselves with the Divine Ground, which is of the same nature as the spirit within.

   We can choose to evolve our spiritual self to become united with the Divine Ground (whatever we consider the divine). Different faiths will vary in their teachings as to the nature of this unity; it can be variously described as, for example, in full unity with, meeting with, returning to, or becoming part of.

4. A human being's life on earth has only one purpose – to identify one's self with one's eternal self, and so come to unitive knowledge of the Divine Ground.

So humankind's purpose is to evolve to spirit and unity with God or Divine Ground. The purpose of our lives is to evolve in order to become nearer to, or more like, or to return to, whatever we call the divine.

Although the perennial philosophy speaks about the divine, some later writers have coined the term 'neo-perennialism', translating 'divine' as 'something bigger', so that the philosophy includes atheistic spirituality. In neo-perennialism, the love of a child, nature, family, and other things of this world, can be that something bigger.

Finding the common ground between world religions is an appealing ideal; it feels like it would move us closer to mutual understanding. But we do have to be careful that in the rush to middle ground we don't discard the details of each tradition without consideration, nor water down their teachings so that we may make a mish-mash of unrelated concepts.

In psychology, the presumption that the middle ground is to be preferred over either extreme is what's called a 'cognitive heuristic'; a type of faulty reasoning, or mental rule of thumb, that we can fall prey to. When we are not sure of something, the middle ground seems fairest or wisest; but this ignores the fact that one option may be more accurate or correct than the other.

Beneath the faith in the middle ground lies the unconscious presumption that each extreme is of equal validity, and that therefore we will find the fulcrum at the centre. But sometimes the belief that the middle ground is truest is mistaken. There are presumably many teachings that are completely man-made, and have much more to do with the human ego and territorialism than God; as such, these teachings need to be not only diluted, but also relegated to the history books.

Our spiritual evolution will need a whole new mainstreaming of spiritual education from early childhood, to equip the person with a vocabulary that the current generation doesn't have. This will involve a counterbalancing of personal rights with personal responsibility in our collective psyche. It will mean a renewed valuation of self-discipline, and a training of the eye outwards in service of the other. It will mean the integration of spiritual practises and aspects into every part of our daily lives. It will require a new paradigm of health that incorporates the human search for meaning.

If the religions of the world are to be part of this spiritual future, some will need to change and modernise the art, symbolism and language used in their teachings. They will need to find ways to go out and speak with the people that feel relevant to the times.

As Aldous Huxley described in his perennial philosophy, one of the unifying themes – taught in various ways by all the faith traditions – is that humankind's ultimate evolution is in spirit. It is towards this full flourishing of our being that we must work – the whole seven days of our week.

**'Truth is one, though sages call it
by many names.'**

– Indian Vedas

18
The Gathering Voices of Oneness
The Goal of Humankind Is Unity

'The God who existed before any religion counts on you to make the oneness of the human family known and celebrated.'

– **Archbishop Desmond Tutu**

Most of us want to live a meaningful life – a purposeful life connected to something more than ourselves. Almost every world religion has teachings on the goal of humanity, and for the spiritual but not religious, the goal is the same as it is for the religious – enlightenment, Nirvana, full flourishing of being, putting on the mind of Christ, the coming of the cosmic Christ, seeing clearly, divinisation, becoming pure love. Each of these are different ways of expressing the end point in our ultimate evolution. This telos is not some vague notion, or future dream to sit and wait for – it is a collective responsibility. It is as vast a task as it is a promise.

'We formed you into tribes and nations so that you might know one another.'

– Qu'ran

Seeing our oneness is not easy. What exactly is oneness? Does it mean that we are connected at source, like rays of light coming from the sun? Does it mean that we belong to the same source, much like three dogs on separate leads are not one dog, but share the same owner? Does it refer to the fact that everything we see in the physical world is created by energy, so that if we were able to map the energy in the world, we would see nothing but energy, with no differentiation – just energy everywhere? Is it sameness, or mutual acceptance? What does oneness mean?

In our material world one person's eating doesn't feed the hungry. One person's happiness does not cause everyone else to smile. So what then? Oneness has become something of a buzzword with the advent of Eastern wisdom teachings into our vocabulary. But with the filters of our senses we can only try to mentally know this oneness; we cannot yet understand it, nor can we see it. Much like someone who is colour-blind accepts that a colour palette exists which they cannot see, some of us are perhaps beginning to accept that we are all connected, in a unitedness we cannot perceive nor fully understand. Even those less sure of our ultimate connectedness are willing to acknowledge that learning to accept each other is good for humanity.

'Star Trek was an attempt to say that humanity will reach maturity and wisdom on the day that it begins not just to tolerate, but take a special delight in differences in ideas and differences in life forms . . .. If we cannot learn to actually enjoy those small differences, to take a positive delight in those small differences between our own kinds, here on this planet, then we do not deserve to go out into space and meet the diversity that is almost certainly there.'
        – Gene Roddenberry, Creator of *Star Trek*

Oneness has been taught since very ancient times. The Stoics considered humankind to be a microcosm of a larger macrocosm, where the cosmos was a single whole, and all living things were manifestations of varying stages of 'pneuma' – a fiery breath which was later thought of as the breath of life or God. For the Stoics, every human soul is a fragment of a universal divine force from which has been partially separated. St Augustine, a very influential Christian writer, described God as being ultimate unity, working down towards the increased materialism and differentiation that we know in our everyday lives.

Plato's allegory of the cave is probably one of the earliest and most famous attempts to teach us that the purpose of our lives is to learn to see further than the eye can see, to look beyond the obviousness, the matter-of-factness of the material world. In his allegory, Plato describes Socrates telling a story about slaves, chained in a cave all of their lives in such a way that they are never able to see outside the cave. The slaves are shackled at their feet and necks. They cannot turn around, and the only way they can 'see' is by way of the shadows thrown onto the wall in front of them by a fire behind them.

Between the slaves and the fire behind them is a raised walkway along which people walk carrying various items above their heads, such as animals, vegetables, plants, wood and stone. A low wall along the side of the walkway hides the shadow of the people carrying the items, so that the slaves only see the shadow of what is being carried, and they associate the sounds they hear with those items.

So, we have the wall of the cave in front of the slaves, then the slaves who cannot turn around, then a walkway behind the slaves, and behind that a fire which casts the shadows of the walkway on the wall in front of the slaves. The slaves, who have never seen the actual plants, animals, and other things being carried directly – instead only their shadow on the wall in front of them – begin a guessing game, where they try to guess which shadow will appear next. Anyone who guessed correctly would become honoured among the group.

One day, a slave is unshackled and forcibly dragged

out of the cave into the daylight. At first he is completely blinded by the light, and can only see by way of shadows and reflections in water or gentle moonlight. But gradually his eyes acclimatise to sunlight, and he learns to see things not as shadows, but in their full form. At first he is shocked by what he sees, but gradually he comes to understand that his former view of reality was wrong – that the sun, not the fire, is the real source of light in the world, and he eventually comes to an appreciation of the stars and the earth.

The slave returns to the cave to tell the others what he has learned. He struggles to get used to the darkness of the cave and to convince the others that what they are seeing is not the full truth. They mock him, seeing his inability to cope with the darkness of the cave as proof that it doesn't pay to go up into the light. Tired of his lecturing, they plot to kill him.

In philosophical circles, Plato's allegory has become hugely famous as a story about our education in the nature of reality. The slaves in the cave who honour the person who guesses the shadows correctly represent the society that is not seeing reality as it truly is but instead honours those who succeed in our limited view of the world.

The slaves, like most of us today, believe that what we see and hear is true, that it is true reality. The sun in the story represents philosophical truth, which Plato said we can only get to by discussion and philosophical education, rather than through our senses. But society does not want to be told that it is merely seeing shadows of reality, even when offered the opportunity to see clearly. The fate of the returning slave is the fate of those who try to show others the truth.

Centuries later in the 200s AD, Plotinus developed Plato's thinking further into what became known as Neoplatonism. Plotinus also wrote about oneness, the division of the soul into two parts, one part divine, the other full of the human passions. He held the view that the senses shape and filter the world around us, rather than passively taking in information, just as Plato had said before him. For centuries since, this question of the limitations of our senses has been a favourite theme for philosophers and psychologists such as Immanuel Kant, William James and others. For them as for the theologians, seeing clearly is the apex of the evolution of humanity.

> **'The plurality that we perceive is only an appearance; it is not real.'**
>
> **– Erwin Schrödinger, Austrian Nobel Prize-winning physicist**

Teachings around oneness, the ultimate unity of everything and seeing clearly are intimately connected; when we un-train our senses from the materialism of the world as we perceive it, we will shed the limitations and filters of our perceptual abilities, and begin to see that all is one, ultimate reality or God. In fact, some Christian writers have said that this is the true meaning of heaven; that heaven is not a place we go to, but instead earth becomes heaven when humankind 'puts on the mind of Christ' by becoming fully loving, and learning to see our unity more clearly. In this thinking, heaven occurs when we lose our human sense of time, and instead step into eternity, which might be timelessness rather than the 'foreverness' that we normally understand it to be. In this understanding, when we die we simply shed the limitations of the body and human time, and the unlovingness of human nature.

'The notion that all these fragments are separately existent is evidently an illusion, and this illusion cannot do other than lead to endless conflict and confusion. Indeed, the attempt to live according to the notion that the fragments are really separate is, in essence, what has led to . . . pollution, destruction of the balance of nature, overpopulation, worldwide economic and political disorder and the creation of an overall environment that is neither physically nor mentally healthy.'
– David Bohm, physicist,
Wholeness and the Implicate Order

Oneness tends to conjure up an image in our minds of becoming that general soup of souls, a blob of disintegrated egos, where nothing is left of what makes us who we are.

But if we think about our children, our family or our friends for a moment, we can see just how wrong it would be to make each of them a carbon copy of ourselves or each other. Our families and friendships flourish when each person feels safe enough to grow to be fully who they are, fully different. A healthy, loving relationship does not require two people to blend into one another. Wouldn't it be more appropriate in church weddings to light a third candle, to represent the new dimension of the newly joined couple, but not extinguish the two candles that represent their individuality?

Trees on a skyline can sway towards each other while also growing up towards the same sun, but still stay separately rooted in the soil. That is the flexible fullness of being oneself that is needed to love.

'The Unprecedented Grandeur of the Phenomenon of Man'

This understanding of unity as a grand collation of each of us was a fundamental teaching of Pierre Teilhard de Chardin, a Jesuit priest and famous palaeontologist in the early 1900s.

Teilhard was one of the discoverers of what became known as 'Peking Man', a set of around forty pre-human fossils dating back to before the evolution of homo erectus, which were hugely important in developing our modern understanding of the evolution of humanity. But what is so unique about Teilhard is the way he connected his scientific understanding of the evolution of earth with his religious beliefs. Far from his scientific knowledge undermining his beliefs, Teilhard believed that science and spirituality had to meet at a common vision. With this in mind, he developed a theory of evolution of humankind that integrated what we now know about humanity's evolution thus far, with a wider lens that foresaw our future evolution towards a type of collective consciousness which he called 'the Omega Point'.

Teilhard was writing not long after Darwin's publication of his theory of evolution, which had gained widespread public acceptance. The challenges of scientific findings which contradicted the teachings of the Roman Catholic Church were already causing tension, and were forefront in the minds of the Vatican hierarchy. Teilhard's writing was interpreted as siding with the scientists. He was banned from serving mass or returning to his native France by the church hierarchy, and also banned from publishing his ideas.

Teilhard was deeply hurt by his exile and frustrated by the prohibition of speaking about his work. He enjoyed a successful scientific career but died of a stroke in New York, still wounded by the hostility he had suffered from the church he so loved.

Teilhard's brilliance, seemingly missed by the Catholic hierarchy, was his ability to fuse the scientific findings on human evolution to date with a view of its future unfolding. His work gave him a sense of awe for what he called 'the unprecedented grandeur of the phenomenon of man', and the interconnectedness of everything.

In Teilhard's view, we, and every atom in existence, are a key component of the whole. All the mundane tasks of our daily lives were for Teilhard a necessary stage in our transformation towards our ultimate spiritual end in the Omega Point. To him, it was the intention behind the way we carry out our daily business that forms the training ground for our divinisation, each task an exercise in which we develop our hearts and minds.

For the atheistic reader, this 'divinisation' might be equivalent to our evolution towards our highest capabilities of love. Keeping in mind that the words 'holy' and 'whole' come from the same stem (the Greek word 'holos'), divinisation is a whole-making process that we must all be a part of. Without each of us, it is not whole.

'All differences in this world are of degree and not kind, because oneness is the secret of everything.'
– Swami Vivekananda (Hindu teacher)

Through his work, Teilhard began to develop a picture of the lifespan of humanity, from the hominisation of earth (when humans first inhabited the planet), which was the focus of his scientific research, forward towards what he considered its ultimate goal. He saw the world as being in a process of evolution, a 'genesis' or upwards trend of matter and spirit towards ultimate unification in the Omega Point.

According to Teilhard, this evolutionary process is to be achieved by the perfecting of ourselves through love. Being a palaeontologist, he describes the geological evolution of the earth in terms of geological layers or zones, beginning with the central metallic barysphere or core, which is enveloped by the rocky lithosphere, which is in turn surrounded by the fluid layers of the hydrosphere and then atmosphere. Added to this is the later development of the flora and fauna or biosphere.

The coming of humankind to earth represented a new leap into thought, from the purely instinctual abilities of the early animal kingdom. And it will be humanity's ability to think, reflect, and self-direct our own thoughts and actions that will, Teilhard believed, create the next layer to be added to the evolution of planet earth; a layer of consciousness and thought which he called the 'noosphere'.

Humanity's existence on the planet, in Teilhard's view, was of far greater importance than being simply another layer of evolution. To him, humanity represented a complete change to the evolution of the planet. Not only does the earth, he says, get a new skin, it also finds its soul. And just as the smallest known elements of our world naturally arrange themselves into larger systems – as molecules do into cells – all of thought will ultimately also join together in a 'mega-synthesis': a unification of the universe which, for Teilhard, was in God.

Teilhard's idea of a noosphere developing around the earth was not completely out of the blue. In 1911, a Ukrainian mineralogist had also suggested that our planet was moving towards its third stage of development. For Vladimir Vernadsky, the previous stages of geosphere and biosphere had been completed, and the earth was beginning to develop a new sphere of pure conscious awareness – a vast system of information similar to the evolution of the cerebral cortex in humans.

In a different vein, modern innovator Elon Musk touched on a similar idea when he spoke about the development of a wireless brain computer system he called 'neural lace', something like Teilhard's noosphere, but formed by technology rather than love.

Arriving at oneness, unity, or Teilhard's Omega Point requires us all to grow outwards towards each other. In Teilhard's world view, we find ourselves once again at the importance of self-transcendence. In self-transcendence we lose ourselves in something greater than ourselves, which includes us rather than dilutes us. We become part of something more. This idea that life continuously extends itself in an unending act of growth is not just a theological teaching:

'Blind indeed are those who do not see the sweep of a movement whose orbit infinitely transcends the natural sciences and has successively invaded and conquered the surrounding territory – chemistry, physics, sociology and even mathematics and the history of religions. One after the other all the fields of human knowledge have been shaken and carried away by the same underwater current in the direction of the study of some development . . . and the definitive access of consciousness to a scale of new dimensions.'

– Carl Jung

Carl Gustav Jung: Psychiatrist and Psychoanalyst

Carl Jung was one of the most influential writers in the history of psychology. He was interested in the spirituality of the individual, but also a 'collective unconscious', a part of each of us that is not individual, but is instead a piece of the whole of humanity. In Jung's eyes, each of us holds a very ancient, inherited connection to all of humankind, the whole of which actually holds us.

Jung insisted that Christ was only one symbol of many for the cosmic unity within us, and that we have to get behind, or look deeper into, the foundations of our consciousness to find the 'eternal ground of all empirical being'. Jung felt that this divine ground can be found by many paths, by anyone, when we come to know, beyond all doubt, that reality as we see it has a transcendent background.

Jung believed that we have to reintegrate the conscious with the collective unconscious, and that when this is done on a universal scale, humanity will become a community of realised selves, a process he called 'individuation'. Jung said he could not tell if God and the unconscious mind are two different entities, but that both are concepts of the transcendent. He urged us all to look for the peacemaker that dwells in the human heart and puts the responsibility for peace on each of us individually – because change must begin somewhere.

'Nobody can afford to look around and wait for somebody else to do what he is loath to do himself. As nobody knows what he could do, he might be bold to ask himself whether by any chance his unconscious might know something helpful, when there is no satisfactory conscious answer anywhere in sight.'

– Carl Jung

The famous American poet and humanist Walt Whitman believed that the apex of humanity's evolution lay at arriving to a spiritual democracy, a time when we would find a common pathway to truth, which could be shared by all. In some of his unpublished writing, Whitman described how each of us can pass through one or all of the religious traditions, to the homogeneous atmosphere of the clear sky above them, where all previous distinctions are lost and we come together.

> **'Is there going to be one heart to the globe? Is humanity forming en-masse?'**
> **– Walt Whitman,** *Leaves of Grass*

We may not yet be at the stage of arriving in those clear skies above the differentiation of religions and atheistic spiritual traditions, but perhaps on our way there we can achieve the spiritual pluralism described by the Dalai Lama, where each of our spiritual lives is viewed as one of many ways to understand ultimate questions about our existence.

This has to mean – as the Dalai Lama asserted – the inclusion of all faiths and none, where that aspect of the person that strives for understanding, meaning, and mattering is recognised and valued.

Love is the challenge and language of this pluralism. None of us have the answers, but we do have the way. Love is more than enough to be getting on with. In doing, we become.

19
Final Thoughts

In *The Seven-Day Soul*, I have tried to share with you my view of spirituality as being part and parcel of our humanity. I hope that I have been as welcoming for the religious reader as for the spiritual but not religious reader, in equal measure.

For too long now the tide of thought has forced our spiritual identities into the shadows, as if in fear of being judged unscientific. But spirituality is not in competition with science. They are each different ways of understanding.

Spirituality is deeply personal, but it must not be left a private enterprise. What we are made of matters, and we must reclaim our spiritual intelligence to design a society that *consciously chooses to nurture what is good*. We must have the courage to strip love of its fluffy labels, and place it firmly at the centre of societal design and public discourse.

Together it is our responsibility to develop society's spiritual vocabulary, with which we can create a map of ourselves. This map can at least point us towards our inner and outer life, the environmental and transcendent dimensions of our being, and the greater contexts in which we exist.

With greater spiritual understanding will come new duties of care towards others and the planet. It will bring us new responsibilities, alongside new rights. It will bring us the deep joy of meaning to animate our daily lives as we reach to fulfil the ultimate goal of humankind. This will be our modern pilgrimage.

But the promises of spiritual wellbeing are not for some more evolved, distant generation. Spiritual education will offer us a new way of seeing the world as it already is and the humdrum aspects of our lives will offer us the repetitions we need to achieve this new world view. When we cosy in to a deeper comfort with the spiritual aspect of ourselves, we will find meaning in the mundane, and courage in confusion; we will notice the beauty of the world around us; and we shall be bowled into silence

Acknowledgements

While I was writing this book, I stuck a note to myself on the wall in front of my desk. It read: 'Thoughts don't type'. The ideas for this book and the things I wanted to say would have continued to wander about inside my head were it not for the fabulous team at Hachette publishing. From Ciara Doorley's enthusiastic response that encouraged me to pull together my ideas, Adrienne Murphy's thought-provoking edits and Elaine Egan and Joanna Smyth's marketing expertise, that ensured this book arrived in to your hands wherever you might be. To them and all the talented team of designers and proof readers, thank you. My sincerest thanks to my publisher Ciara Considine, who has shown endless patience, compassionate encouragement and a skilled hand in bringing this book to fruition. Thank you.

To Sr. Mary Hilary Daly and Sr. Stanislaus Kennedy, who both embody the openness, stillness and forgiveness typical of a mature faith, thank you.

To all my contributors, whether or not your name has been changed, thank you for sharing your experiences with us all.

To An tUachtarán na hÉireann Michael D. Higgins, thank you for your generous contribution and your beautiful illumination of the many ways of understanding available to us. Thanks to Hans Zomer, in the office of the President of Ireland, for all your kind work on my behalf – it is hugely appreciated.

To all the great thinkers and scientists upon whose work this book is built – thank you.

And to all my family, particularly my husband and our three boys: you have been unendingly patient and forgiving in allowing me the time to disappear far more than I should have, to complete this book. I cannot thank you all enough for your selfless, loving support. You are my heroes. Can I take this opportunity to put to rest once and for all a certain question: Mum loves *you* more. To the moon and back is just the beginning.

Bibliography

(For a full bibliography and recommendations please visit www.susannahhealy.com)

Chapter 2: Perception Deception
HRH The Prince of Wales, with Juniper, T. and Skelly, I. 2010. *Harmony: A New Way of Looking at Our World.* Blue Door

Chapter 3: Images of God
Catechism of the Catholic Church. Part 1: The Profession of Faith. Section 1, Chapter 1 (IV): 42

Fowler, James. 1995. *Stages of Faith: The Psychology of Human Development and the Quest for Meaning.* Bravo Publishing, new edition (originally published in 1981)

Chapter 4: The Seven Pillars
The inspirational quote by Joe Schmidt was reported by ex-Irish rugby international Paul O'Connell at Pendulum Summit, 2018

Chapter 5: The Vertical Axis
Kabat-Zinn, J. 1991. *Full Catastrophe Living: How To Cope with Stress, Pain and Illness Using Mindfulness Meditation.* Piatkus

Keating, T. 2006. *Open Heart, Open Mind.* Bloomsbury Publishing

Chapter 6: Do We End at Our Epidermis?
Costello, S. 2011. *The Ethics of Happiness: An Existential Analysis.* Wyndham Hall Press

Frankl, V. 2000. *Man's Search For Ultimate Meaning.* Perseus Publishing

Chapter 8: Expanding Our Gears of Consciousness
McGilchrist, I. 2009. *The Master and His Emissary: The Divided Brain and the Making of the Western World.* Yale University Press

Chapter 9: Spirituality in Parenting and Family Life
Keating, N. 2018. *Meditation with Children: A Resource for Teachers and Parents.* Veritas

Chapter 10: Further, Higher, Deeper
Foster Wallace, D. 2004. *Consider the Lobster and Other Essays.* Little, Brown & Co. Fredrickson, B.L., Grewan, K.M., Coffey, K.A., Algoe, S.B., Firestine, A.M., Arevalo, J.M.G., Ma, J., Cole,

S.W. 2013. 'A Functional Genomic Perspective on Human Well-Being', *Proceedings of the National Academy of Sciences of the United States of America*. 13 August: 110 (33): 13684–9

Chapter 11: Inhaling the Breadth of Meaning

Ariely, D., Kamenica, E., Prelec, D. 2008. 'Man's Search for Meaning: The Case of Legos'. *Economic Behavior and Organization*. 67: 671–7

The example of Medtel is discussed in a report by The Fetzer Institute. See www.fetzer.org

Chapter 13: Spirituality in Education

International Commission on Education for the Twenty-first Century, Delors, J. and UNESCO. 1996. *Learning: The Treasure Within. Report to UNESCO of the International Commission on Education for the Twenty-first Century*. UNESCO Pub.

Chapter 14: Spirituality in Government

Ahern, B. as cited in Waters, J. 2008. *Lapsed Agnostic*. Bloomsbury

Chapter 15: Spirituality in Healthcare

Fisher, J. 2011. 'The Four Domains Model: Connecting Spirituality, Health and Well-Being'. *Religions*. 2 (1): 17–28

Puchalski, C.M. 2001. 'The Role of Spirituality in Health Care'. *Baylor University Medical Center Proceedings*. 14 (4): 352–7

Chapter 16: The Spirit of Our Spaces

Kaplan, R., Kaplan, S. 1995. *The Experience of Nature: A Psychological Perspective*. University of Washington Press

Amicone, G., Petruccelli, I., De Dominicis, S., et al. 2018. 'Green Breaks: The Restorative Effect of the School Environment's Green Areas on Children's Cognitive Performance'. *Frontiers in Psychology*. 9: 1579

Rose, K.A., French, A., Morgan, I.G., Mitchell, P. 2012. 'Incidence of Myopia in Australian Adolescents: The Sydney Childhood Eye Study (SCES)'. ARVO Annual Meeting Abstract. www.ccities.org

Chapter 18: The Gathering Voices of Oneness

Teilhard de Chardin, P. 2008. *The Phenomenon of Man*. Harper Perennial (first English ed. 1959)